DUBLIN

By Brendan Lehane
and the Editors of Time-Life Books

With Photographs by John McDermott
and Laurie Lewis

THE GREAT CITIES · TIME-LIFE BOOKS · AMSTERDAM

The Author: Brendan Lehane was born in London of Irish parents in 1936. After graduation from Cambridge University, he worked for two years on magazines and in book publishing, travelled for a year in Africa, and then became a freelance writer. His books include *The Companion Guide to Ireland*, *The Quest of Three Abbots* (about Ireland in the 6th and 7th Centuries), *The Compleat Flea* and *The Power of Plants*.

The Photographers: John McDermott is of Irish extraction and was born in Philadelphia in 1947. He graduated from the University of Wisconsin and has worked as a photographer in San Francisco since 1975. He is a contributor to major U.S. magazines, including *Time* and *Sports Illustrated*.

Born in London, Laurie Lewis studied at the Royal College of Art, London, and at the University of California, Los Angeles. He has worked on a number of documentary films, covering events such as the turbulent 1968 Democratic Convention in Chicago and the volcanic eruption in Heimaey, off Iceland, in 1973. His work has also appeared in TIME-LIFE Books, *Rolling Stone* magazine and other publications.

TIME-LIFE INTERNATIONAL
EUROPEAN EDITOR: George Constable
Assistant European Editor: Kit van Tulleken
Design Consultant: Louis Klein
Chief Designer: Graham Davis
Director of Photography: Pamela Marke
Chief of Research: Vanessa Kramer

THE GREAT CITIES
Series Editor: Simon Rigge

Editorial Staff for *Dublin*
Deputy Editor: Christopher Farman
Designers: Derek Copsey, Joyce Mason
Picture Editor: Jasmine Spencer
Staff Writers: Tony Allan, Mike Brown
Text Researchers: Liz Goodman, Elizabeth Loving
Design Assistant: Mary Staples

Editorial Production
Production Editor: Ellen Brush
Art Department: Julia West
Editorial Department: Ajaib Singh Gill, Joanne Holland
Picture Department: Lynn Farr, Gina Marfell, Belinda Stewart Cox

The captions and the texts accompanying the photographs in this volume were prepared by the editors of TIME-LIFE Books.

Published by TIME-LIFE International (Nederland) B.V. Ottho Heldringstraat 5, Amsterdam 1018.

© 1978 TIME-LIFE International (Nederland) B.V. All rights reserved. Second English printing, 1979.

ISBN 7054 0498 6

Cover: Atop a lamp-post, the wrought-iron tendrils of a shamrock, Ireland's national emblem, frame an ivy-clad façade in Dublin's Merrion Square. The houses around the square were built in the 18th Century for the Anglo-Irish aristocrats who then dominated the city's affairs—and who remained the ruling élite until after the First World War.

First end paper: Gleaming like candles on an altar, brass beer pump handles in one of Dublin's five hundred or so pubs offer promise of the city's most famous refreshment—a foam-capped "jar" of locally brewed Guinness.

Last end paper: Drawn by a pair of spritely stags, Diana the Huntress adorns a ceiling at Belvedere House, one of the 18th-Century mansions that gave Dublin its reputation for architectural splendour. The house was later converted into a Jesuit boys' school, and it was here that the young James Joyce won first prize for English composition.

Contents

I

The Chameleon City

Seen from the sea, Dublin keeps you guessing up to the last moment. There is a lighthouse, a factory chimney, an office block, and the squat cylinder of the city's main gas-storage tank. The rest, until you are close, is a long, low line of shadow, like an unpromising mirage. To the left rise the green and purple mountains of County Wicklow; on the right stands the complacent hump of the northern promontory, Howth Head. You could not be expected to guess, if you did not already know, that between these two bosomy outgrowths of rock is spread Ireland's capital city, 45 square miles of asphalt, stone and brick containing some 750,000 souls—nearly a third of the Republic's population and a similar proportion of its man-made grandeur. None of this is evident from the sea lanes. Judging from all the outward signs she displays, Dublin might not be at home today.

She is at home, as you see once you disembark—at home, and trying on an outfit from her roomy wardrobe, matching her appearance to the season and the colour of the sky. There are days of bluster and cold drizzle, when the streets glower in a mantle of black and grey. There are days of blue and gold, when the great public buildings of the 18th Century luxuriate in their mellowed splendour, and miles of more modest houses warm to intimacy as their fabric breathes in the sunlight. And there are days in between, when Dublin changes a dozen times to match successive, subtle gradings of the atmosphere. Like many of her inhabitants, Celtic and mercurial, she is a bit of a chameleon.

It is the variety of costume, and the many facets of her citizens, that make me nervous in approaching the subject. The printing process will in due course efface the tremolo of my handwriting, but it will not alter the apprehension I feel on trying to convert a capital city—a complex amalgam of past, present, people, passion, peace, war, pedantry and *badinage*—into a few thousand words of print. The problem applies to any city but to Dublin, I think, more than most. For one thing, the bars and garrets of Dublin are crowded with writers, each with a ready portrait of his native town, each primed to snap like a trap on literary trespassers. And there are other snares. Compared with London, Paris or New York (each of which has a population at least ten times greater), Dublin is small, compact, and neatly circumscribed: by sea to the east, mountains to the south, and pastures to north and west. Smallness being easily taken for simplicity, Dublin invites dogmatic statement and generalization. It seems on first sight to be a nice, assimilable, pocket-size town that behaves, like a model railway, exactly as one thought it would. Any package theory about

Silhouetted in the sunlight of a bright December day, Christmas shoppers crowd Grafton Street, where many of Dublin's most fashionable stores and shops are located. Dubliners enjoy frequent interludes in their jaunts to the area— exchanging gossip over coffee in Bewley's Café, the tall building to the right of the bus, or over something stronger in the many nearby bars.

it can be supported by evidence on the ground. Any visitor will find his picture of the city fits neatly into the nutshell of reality, and he may well go away unaware that this particular nutshell happens to contain an infinite number of kernels.

Of one thing there is no doubt: Dublin's greatness is a palpable quality, not subject to the whims or bias of the observer. No one would deny that the city has been a nursery of great literature, nourishing some of the most distinguished and influential writers in the Western world: the poet William Butler Yeats, holding reality up to the myriad facets of his tirelessly analytical mind; the novelist James Joyce, subjecting Dublin—and through it mankind—to the cynical lens of his mental microscope; the playwrights Richard Brinsley Sheridan, John Millington Synge, Sean O'Casey, George Bernard Shaw, Oscar Wilde; the clerical satirist Jonathan Swift, author of *Gulliver's Travels*; Bram Stoker, creator of Dracula; Brendan Behan, in his short life almost a walking definition of Irish blarney; and scores more.

The accomplishments of Dublin's writers are rivalled by those of her architects. Buildings as grand as any in Europe break the skyline on either side of the River Liffey. In its eastward flow through the city, the river passes within half a mile of almost all of them. Kilmainham Royal Hospital, four-square and stately, dominates the western approaches of Dublin as it has since 1684. Closer to the centre, on the north-bank quays, stands the massive 18th-Century Four Courts building, Ireland's judicial head-quarters, with its four chambers radiating from the central lantern-dome.

On the other side of the river, and on high ground, is Christ Church Cathedral, the oldest building in Dublin, dating from the 12th Century and—thanks to 19th-Century restoration—a still-sound Gothic colossus flaunting its pinnacles and flying buttresses. A second cathedral, St. Patrick's, rises a quarter of a mile south of Christ Church, and presents a less florid, more endearing profile, though it was begun 20 years after its elevated sister. Down river, and again on the south side, is the baroque dome of the City Hall, distinguished more for size than beauty; and behind it are the rambling courtyards of Dublin Castle, built by successive British viceroys in an assortment of styles, so that bald medieval stone towers abut on the mannered redbrick of the 18th Century.

Half a mile downstream, the broad artery of O'Connell Street leads north from the river, to end at the curved colonnade of the Rotunda—18th-Century assembly rooms that now contain a theatre auditorium and a cinema. Opposite, on the river's south side, but hidden from it by workaday buildings on the quays, are two of Dublin's prime monuments. The Bank of Ireland, originally built to house Ireland's parliament, presents a dramatic sweep of columns, bone-white from their first cleaning in 1977, and leads the eye to the focal thoroughfare of College Green; opposite, the long grey façade of Trinity College hides two spacious quadrangles and a treasury of architecture and sculpture. Then, before

Trapped in a changing world, a cart-driver tries to manoeuvre through a Dublin traffic jam. Horse-drawn carts were commonplace in the city until the 1960s.

the river flows through nondescript docks and outskirts to the sea, there rises on the north the crowning glory of the Custom House, massively domed like the Four Courts, but in a lighter, more feminine form.

Like many women of the Irish countryside, Dublin is a great beauty wrapped in a tattered shawl. Between the peaks of her grander buildings, alongside green parks and exquisitely proportioned rows of houses, are troughs of slumland, bleak wastes disfigured by huge advertising billboards hiding half-fallen or demolished buildings that nobody has the will or money to replace. Most of the grandeur dates from long before 1921, when the Irish won their independence after more than seven hundred years of English rule. The care in erecting buildings, in framing vistas, in conjuring settings to please the eye was the achievement of English settlers and their descendants, a foreign plant that is now dying as the iron of its hothouse rusts and the glass falls and breaks.

Modern Dublin sometimes seems blind to its heritage. Eighteenth-Century buildings, which in England or almost anywhere in Western Europe would be swathed with notices advertising their history and times of opening, here remain tattered, patched, crudely adapted to new functions. All over the city, 18th-Century façades are obscured, or their proportions mangled, by neon-lit plastic signs. Even the columned quadrant of the Rotunda is partly obliterated by brash advertisements for the films being shown within.

Over front doors, plaster saints or images of Pope John and President Kennedy (both of whom would be sainted instantly if it were left to an Irish vote) look out from semi-elliptical or rectangular fanlights whose designers would have deplored such visual clutter, let alone the religious sentiments. Old men in raincoats snore on iron seats skilfully wrought by Victorian craftsmen. Beneath converted Victorian gas lamps, beside huge cast-iron post-boxes still bearing the letters VR, initials of the Queen under whose dominion they were erected, above cobbles and antique granite pavings—some of them chipped away, flake by flake, by masons to accommodate decorative coal-hole covers—Dublin passes unheeding. To the despair of aesthetic purists, Dublin refuses to turn herself into a museum. She is more heart than head, and antiquarians can go hang.

But there is a perverse and unintended taste in the tastelessness of the place. Dublin's lack of style is in itself a style. Certain sights and smells seem to be eternal, incontrovertible, essential to the city's character: the reek of stale beer emanating from pubs and of urine from under bridges and decrepit gateways; the tetchy moodiness of winds that rise suddenly from torpor and blow papers and bags and discarded cigarette packets across open spaces, around corners, or up into the aerial suspension of invisible whirlpools; a pervasive untidiness and a universal leavening of dirt, noted by travellers for centuries. The phrase "dear, dirty Dublin", first coined by a literary hostess of the 1830s, has stuck.

Conventional Irish pleasures do not include eating well or dressing smartly, or living in nicely designed rooms. The Irish are the despair of the colour supplements. Clothes keep out the weather, food replaces calories, alcohol oils the flow of talk, no matter whether the vessel that brings it to the lips be of glass, pewter or tin. A mouth islanded in a sea of stubble, under nostrils sprouting tuffets of bristle, under hair that shows but a passing acquaintance with the comb—that mouth can talk as well as any other.

Beggars abound, and so do the tinkers, also known euphemistically as travellers or itinerants, a race with similarities to the gipsies of England, but cut off from them (at least until some of them realized that commuting between the two countries could lead to a double dole). Unlike the gipsies, who are believed to have come from Egypt, the tinkers were originally a wandering people of the Irish countryside, and their language, Shelta, developed from Gaelic, the ancient language of Ireland. There are about 200 tinker families in Dublin, and more than half are on-the-road, sly, weather-beaten roughs with a sullen manner of pleading; "chancers and tramps," an Irish writer, Ulick O'Connor, called them, "who'd lift the froth off your pint if you didn't keep your nose well in over the edge of the glass".

Yet, in my middle-class and heartless way, I find them colourful—as I do the other members of the Dublin scene: the drunks and monks, the madmen and evangelists, the pompous new gentry and the visiting priests from faraway lands whose worried looks reflect the difficulty they have in squaring squalor, filth and a pervading unkemptitude with their image of a holy city. England has no town that offers such a range of personal curiosities, though it must have had many in Chaucer's or Hogarth's or Dickens' days. Dublin is usually a little behind the times.

Any of those artists would have made much of Dublin, though today, from boardrooms and municipal offices, a brave new world is threatening to sweep away the nonconformities of the place. Eccentrics, for which Dublin is justly famous, are not quite what they were. There is no one to replace Sir William Wilde, the father of Oscar, most brilliant of Dublin-born wits. Sir William was an eye specialist who succeeded in worsening the squint of Bernard Shaw's father and rummaged in cemeteries for his researches into phrenology; it was said of him that his nails were always dirty because he was always scratching himself. There were others, too, like the 18th-Century Lord Montagu, who to please his mistress spent his mature years aping the imagined conduct and style of an emperor of China; and Buck Whaley, a dandy of the same period, who once jumped from a first-floor window into his carriage seat and travelled to Jerusalem to win a bet; and George Robert Fitzgerald, who on his estate in Galway kept his obstreperous father chained to a pet bear, and hunted rabbits at night by the light of torches.

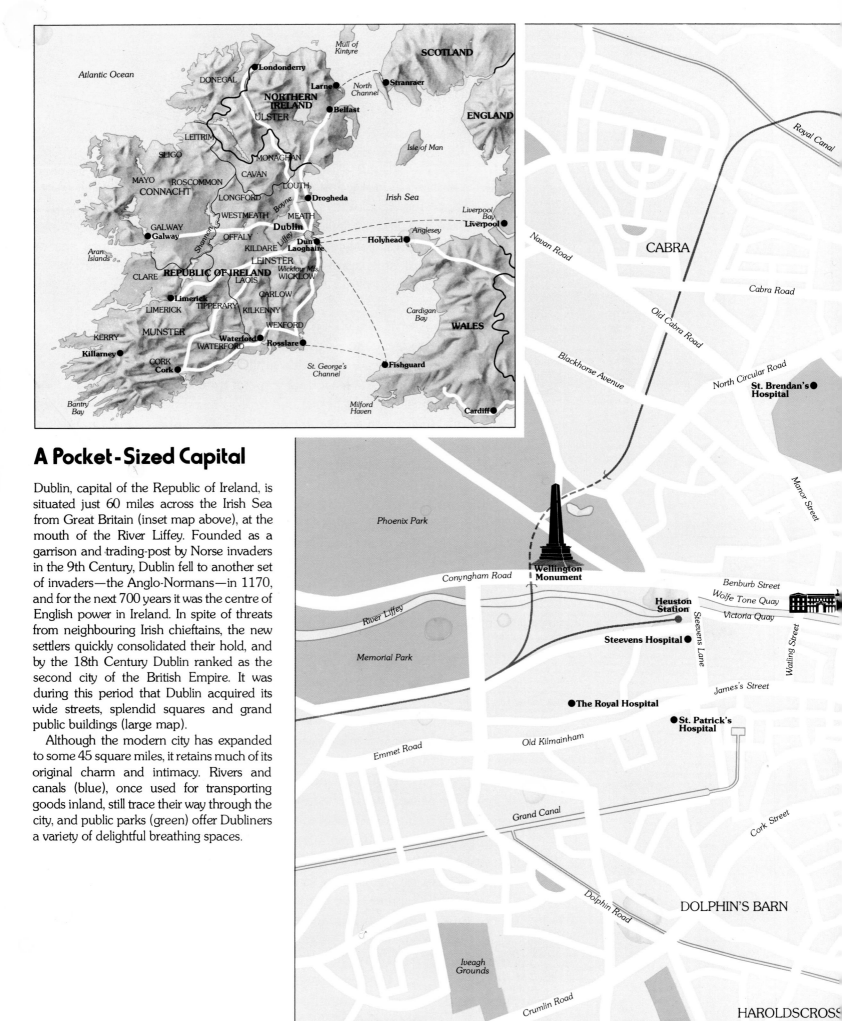

A Pocket-Sized Capital

Dublin, capital of the Republic of Ireland, is situated just 60 miles across the Irish Sea from Great Britain (inset map above), at the mouth of the River Liffey. Founded as a garrison and trading-post by Norse invaders in the 9th Century, Dublin fell to another set of invaders—the Anglo-Normans—in 1170, and for the next 700 years it was the centre of English power in Ireland. In spite of threats from neighbouring Irish chieftains, the new settlers quickly consolidated their hold, and by the 18th Century Dublin ranked as the second city of the British Empire. It was during this period that Dublin acquired its wide streets, splendid squares and grand public buildings (large map).

Although the modern city has expanded to some 45 square miles, it retains much of its original charm and intimacy. Rivers and canals (blue), once used for transporting goods inland, still trace their way through the city, and public parks (green) offer Dubliners a variety of delightful breathing spaces.

Botanic Gardens

GLASNEVIN

DRUMCONDRA

Prospect Cemetery

O'Connell Monument

nglas Road

St. Patrick's Training College

Tolka River

Griffith Avenue

Croyden Gardens

Marino

Clontarf Golf Course

CLONTARF

Philipsburgh Avenue

Marino

Malahide Road

Howth Road

St. Vincent's Hospital ●

Richmond Road

Fairview

Clontarf Road
Clontarf Promenade

Holy Cross College

Clonliffe Road

Fairview Park

Mountjoy Jail ●

PHIBSBOROUGH

Drumcondra Road

Croke Park

Mater Misericordiae Hospital ●

Phibsborough Road

Eccles Street

20 Dominick Street

Mountjoy Square

Constitution Hill

Dominick St.

Dorset Street

Belvedere College

Summerhill

McDermott Street

Amiens Street

Seville Place

King's Inns ●

Henrietta Street

Parnell Statue

Gardiner Street

Foley Street

Connolly Station

Law Library

Rotunda

Parnell Street

Moore St.

O'Connell Street

St. Mary's Pro-Cathedral

Talbot Street

Sheriff Street

ng Street

Capel Street

Mary Street

General Post Office

O'Connell Statue

Liberty Hall ●

Custom House

Mary's Lane

Abbey Street

Abbey Theatre

Butt Bridge

Matt Talbot Bridge

North Wall Quay

Alexandra Basin

Four Courts

Liffey Bridge

Grattan Bridge

O'Connell Bridge

River Liffey

Sir John Rogerson's Quay

her's y

Dame Street

Cork Hill

Bank of Ireland

Townsend Street

Hanover Street

Lighthouse ●

St. Augustine Street

Christ Church Cathedral

City Hall

Dublin Castle

College Green

Grafton Street

Wicklow Street

Trinity College

Pearse Street

Pearse Station

Cambridge Road

Patrick Street

Dublin Civic Museum

Aungier Street

National Library

Molesworth Street

Westland Row

St. Stephen's Church

National Gallery

Ringsend Park

t. Patrick's Cathedral

Marsh's Library

St. Stephen's Green

Leinster House

Merrion Square

Shelbourne Park Greyhound Race Course

Shelbourne Stadium

Cliffe Street

Camden Street

Harcourt Street

Mount Street

River Dodder

IRISHTOWN

BELLEVILLE

Synge Street

Fitzwilliam Square

Fitzwilliam Street

Baggot Street

Lansdowne Rugby Ground

Beach Road

Sandymount Road

Newman House, University College

Leeson Street

Wilton Terrace

SANDYMOUNT

Clanbrasil Street

South Circular Road

Adelaide Road

Grand Canal

Harold's Cross

Rathmines Road

Ranelagh Road

Ranelagh Road

RANELAGH

BALLSBRIDGE

Cathal Brugha Barracks

Herbert Park

Royal Dublin Society

Some lived in our own century, such as "The Bird" Flanagan, as he was always known, who once pretended to steal a ham (which he had in fact paid for) to experience the thrill of a police chase and arrest; and the man known as Endymion, who paced the streets in his white flannel trousers and black tail coat and undersize bowler, carrying sabres with which he saluted people and statues, and an alarm clock and compass with which he frequently verified that the sun rises in the east.

If the great age of eccentrics is past, lesser oddities remain in plenty: the harlequin character, no more than 30, who loafs about in Grafton Street among the shoppers, his face painted with multi-coloured cubes and circles, offering to talk about singularly high-brow matters with anybody who cares to stop; the bald 60-year-old who sits on a bench in the green by St. Patrick's and on a frosty morning exposes a cheery smile and naked bronzed torso to any who pass; the gentleman in an over-large grey suit who walks about the city's south side, animatedly conducting some private orchestra with a sensitive outstretched fore-finger, humming loudly.

True, these are the pickings, figures who stand out because the multitude are not like them. But the average Dubliner is not a natural conformist. It was the coincidence of a visit to Dublin after a stay in clean and orderly Switzerland that showed me the welcome, common-sense anarchy of the Dublin crowd. Here, people rely on eyesight and agility to cross the road rather than waiting beside empty intersections until the traffic lights tell them to walk. Publicans are not always strict in observing legal closing time; and police often turn a blind eye to minor infringements. A prevalent disorder can even be discerned in the everyday noises of Dublin—the banshee wail of a newly introduced model of bus, the insistent screech of badly maintained brakes, the sirens of police, ambulances and fire brigades that make one suspect there is no emergency but merely an excess of bravado in their drivers.

I have not written so far in much fear of contradiction. These sights, sounds and smells are sufficiently well accepted to satisfy Dickens' Mr. Gradgrind, who believed in facts and statistics and nothing else. I have perhaps betrayed my affection for the city in the way I have presented them; and that is as well, for I have loved Dublin as long as I have known her, and that is a fact too. But my Dublin is not yours, and yours is not your neighbour's. Under the façades of the palpable Dublin we see and feel are the many Dublins of illusion and imagination.

At the airports, the quays and the railway stations, microcosmic Dublins arrive daily in the minds of visitors. The English fortify their notions of their own Anglo-Saxon stolidity by pointing out, with told-you-so nods, the more feckless aspects of the natives and the handsome, enduring monuments to what was principally an English regime in Dublin during the 18th Century. The French see holiness writ large in the churches and

Dublin's coat of arms, seen here on a lamppost, dates from the reign of Elizabeth I and is a reminder of British rule. The castle shown in triplicate is believed to represent Dublin Castle, built in 1204, and the flames above the towers may recall fires started by raiding tribesmen in the Middle Ages. The motto reads: "The city's happiness depends on the people's loyalty."

the proliferation of ecclesiastical collars, monks and nuns. Liberal Germans sigh longingly at the apparent viability of a race of happy natural individualists so notably in contrast with the efficiency of the teutonic homeland. Americans find the fun, wit, charm, generosity and blarney their guidebooks have predisposed them to find.

There are those of any nation who, brought up on literary fancies and tales of Liffey water—often falsely described as the secret in Ireland's famous creamy dark stout—come prepared for a kind of Nordic lotusland on the banks of the River Guinness. They are here, in a sense, to see an allegory, a symbol of some innocently hedonistic corner of their minds. Others expect smiling eyes and loquacious good cheer, a better wit than Limehouse or Brooklyn fosters, pretty girls with green eyes and russet hair, and heart-stirring dirges wafting from bar doorways. They will find them. The seller of shoe-laces will say, "That'll be eight pence, if you have it"—as if it doesn't matter if you don't—and the memory will eclipse all less favourable impressions. "Tea?" says the grocer, who also sells tobacco, paperback thrillers, apples and Catholic literature. "Tea? And it gettin' cheaper by the hour. You're on a winner there." The Guinness will go to their heads, and they will unload the cargo of their minds to some bar-propper who will nod with the same rapt attention he would pay to the prophecies of John the Baptist. And in the afterglow—for them —all Dublin will be bathed in the light of that memory. Some will come looking for a kind of 18th-Century sanctuary, for stucco ornaments, fanlights, wing staircases and everything to admire in a Palladian paradise. The physical refinement of the Age of Enlightenment is there to be seen, and if you choose to, you can blot shoddier products out of your mind. Still others will be hunting the Celt, the procrastinating, begorrah-ing, impish, yarn-spinning stage-Irishman; and he too, in spite of vehement denial by serious nationalists, is ubiquitous.

I am reminded of that relaxed Irish aphorism, "Sure, the man who made time made plenty of it"; and of the bus driver who recently arrived an hour late to take a group of us to some seminar in the country. He was balding, but such hair as was prepared to grow floated in waves to his shoulders. He dismounted and stooped before us in abject penitence. Then, with both arms, he made the most eloquent gesture I have ever seen. Not a word did he say, but you could read that gesture like a book. It said: I am emptied, good people, drained of the energy to tell you of it all, of the trials and tribulations I've had to face getting here, the traffic-jams, accidents, road-works, hold-ups, hijacks, the hail and blizzards, the earthquake here and the tidal wave there. Accept my word, my contrition. Sure to God, nothing but His divine intervention would have got me here at all.

The driver had not opened his mouth, and the June day was dull and uneventful. Yet I swear we all felt, as we climbed into the bus, an ineffable pity for the man who, his gesture convinced us, had been to hell and back for our service. If such characters—and they abound—are stage-Irishmen, then Dublin is a theatre.

My own first acquaintance with Dublin was attended by illusions of another kind, though I suppose I have felt, in my time, each of those referred to. Indeed, I doubt if anyone has so earnestly tried to fit the square of his imagination into the round hole of Dublin as much as I. My blood is all Irish, but I was born and bred in England, and from these circumstances I derive a mild schizophrenia. Part of my childhood was passed in north London, where my Catholic Irish father taught in a school run by Jesuits, St. Ignatius' College. My world then was partially formed by priests with Irish accents—my father's colleagues—and boys with Irish names. In a sense the school was part of the Dublin Diaspora, a piece of Ireland adrift in an ocean of English suburbs. I pictured the real Dublin as the Holy City, and peopled it with the kind of pipe-puffing Jesuit I knew—stern, aromatically patriarchal, dustily flesh-denying. Many wore spectacles with thin, dark, round frames, and they spoke with quiet modulations savouring, so it seemed to me, of sadism and sanctimony, which I took to be the ingredients of holiness, and an important part of the Dublin mix.

These were early and somewhat vague impressions, although no less strong for being so. Then something more important came to shape my expectations of Dublin. When I was 13, luck and a precocious enthusiasm for Samuel Johnson (that loquacious 18th-Century essayist who, as it happens, despised the Irish: "a very fair nation—they never speak well of one another") got me a scholarship to Eton, a rather grand boarding-school for what is left of the English aristocracy and those who aspire to it, certainly not for the likes of me.

My primary concern there quickly became a matter of hiding my origins. North London's redbrick avenues were no match for the manors and mansions of my schoolmates. I learned a little cunning, and Dublin—and the Lehane clan's ancient homeland in County Cork—adopted new roles in my life. I spun tales of a ruined family castle (having little idea at the time that one actually existed) and descent from the 11th-Century Celtic High King Brian Boru (quite groundless). I picked up a little Irish history and sniped at my colleagues with snippets of English colonial oppression. There was no fear of contradiction, since the English have never voluntarily paid attention to Ireland, and most know nothing about it whatever. If, as sometimes happened, they became angry, so much the better for me. I was raised from the status of an underprivileged compatriot to the equality of an alien.

My knowledge of the virtues of the Irish grew, since these were useful weapons. Their weaknesses I ignored. Confronted with hackneyed English jibes at the Irish—that they were an illiterate rabble, prone to drink and brawling—I learned to counter, correctly, that of the half-dozen most distinguished "English" dramatists of the last two centuries, at least four

Viewed north-eastwards from the city centre, Dublin stretches towards Fairview Park. The city is expanding to meet a population growth of nearly 10,000 a year.

were Irish; that of the 10 most distinguished generals anyone could think of in English history, more than half were likely to be Irish-born, including the Duke of Wellington, Lord Kitchener, and more recently Field-Marshals Montgomery of Alamein and Alexander of Tunis; and that in ancient times Ireland had helped to keep Christianity alive when her neighbours were overrun by barbarians—a time when many of my high-born companions' ancestors were drunken freebooters, snoring on skins in the frigid caves of Scandinavia.

Dublin, in other words, was becoming an escape, none too firmly based on any reality I knew. My earliest visits were short enough to preserve the image intact. My first prolonged adult visit put it more to the test, and there were days when I seemed to see only dirt, poverty and a smugly bourgeois self-satisfaction. Dublin was holy, to be sure—if holiness is to be judged by the real estate occupied by churches, monasteries, church schools, seminaries and mission headquarters. It contained a higher proportion of nuns, priests and monks to laymen than any place I knew or know; but many of these were so rubicund and portly that they suggested links with Boccaccio more than St. Antony. There were other disillusionments. Some people had charm, were late for things, smiled and often embroidered street directions with winsome similes: a street might be "long as a hare's leg", so long in fact that "ye'll wear out a couple o' pairs o' shoes on that one". But many of these Dubliners used their qualities to evil purpose, like the landlord of one flat I occupied. He belonged to the Knights of Columbanus (a Catholic fraternity named after a 7th-Century Irish missionary) and was thus a pillar of society. Nevertheless, he produced every ruse and hyperbole from the manual of stage-Irishry to deflect my complaints about vermin: he extolled the merits, agility and cunning of fleas so insistently and effectively that I became a flea-admirer and wrote a book about them.

I soon began to discover the constricting qualities that had driven many of Dublin's natives, including some of her greatest writers—James Joyce, Oscar Wilde, Bernard Shaw—into voluntary exile. I heard residents venting their own frustrations. Dublin was a totalitarian state, under the tyranny of her archbishop or of a smug and obscurantist prime minister. Dublin was still run by British imperialism, under the disguise of a lick-spittle Irish government; or, on the other hand, Dublin had been mis-governed by a corrupt and vengeful caucus ever since the Irish took over government from their old masters in 1921.

The Irish seemed greatly to enjoy malicious gossip. No Irishman, somebody has observed, will say anything about you to your face that he would not prefer to say behind your back. The novelist Honor Tracy wrote that members of the race "are great ones for rescuing those they have previously drowned". "If a Dubliner," a resident historian has claimed, "is told any city in the world is as malicious as his, he is seriously put out."

I found myself beginning to agree with such generalizations, at which the Irish are so adept, and which collectively prompted an English prime minister, Herbert Asquith, to make the remark—one of many similar cries of English despair—"You will never get to the bottom of this perplexing and damnable country".

Underneath all the paradox and contradiction lies the confusing fact that while London is and always has been an English town and Paris always French, Dublin was for most of its existence hardly Irish at all. It enters history more than a thousand years ago as a garrison town of the Scandinavian colonists, better known as Vikings or Norsemen, who in the 8th and 9th Centuries were establishing ports and spring-boards for inland plunder all round the coasts of northern Europe. From that time onwards Dublin continued to be a foreign stronghold, with just one brief interlude. In 1014, the Irish rallied under their warrior king Brian Boru, defeated the Norsemen at the village of Clontarf, close to Dublin, and drove them from Dublin itself. But the Norse re-established themselves, and when Dublin changed hands again, the victors were not the Irish but an invasion force of Anglo-Normans who landed in 1169 and began Ireland's long subjection to her more powerful neighbour, England.

This invasion can be seen, from a glance at the map, to be an almost inevitable result of geography. The west coast of Britain reaches out towards Ireland like the clasping talons of a hawk, and the journey across the Irish Sea is no more than 20 miles at the narrowest point. Sooner or later the British were bound to extend their grasp round this vulnerable prey. Once they did, the primary themes of all subsequent Irish history were established.

Dublin was an obvious site for the Anglo-Norman headquarters. It had been well developed as a naval base by the Norsemen, with strong fortresses, wooden houses and storerooms, and a thriving trade in wine and cloth. It afforded easy access by river and road into the interior. The Anglo-Normans colonized it, re-walled it and edified it with fine buildings. From that moment on, the history of Dublin and that of Ireland diverged. Dublin became a predominantly English town, a centre from which English settlers were disseminated to the rest of Ireland.

Until the end of the 16th Century, direct English influence was restricted to a strip of land along the east coast, varying in extent but running roughly from the town of Dundalk, 50 miles away in the north, to a point little farther south than Dublin; the area was known as the English Pale or "the obedient shires". English policy, roughly stated, was to extend the boundaries of the Pale into the dark, barbarian country beyond. During the 17th and 18th Centuries increasing numbers of English Protestant settlers came and did just that. They became the landlords of Ireland, a group sufficiently diluted with Irish blood and Irish ways to have achieved an identity of their own as the Anglo-Irish, and yet sufficiently apart and so much more powerful than the Catholic majority of Ireland to be known also as the Protestant Ascendancy. Eighteenth-Century Dublin, with its fine Palladian houses and grand public buildings, was their capital. To them, it was second only to London or Paris in fashion and social glitter.

After 1921, when Dublin became the capital of the Irish Free State, the influence of the Anglo-Irish declined, but it was not extinguished. Dublin has become more Irish than any English town, yet remains more English than other towns in independent Ireland. Above all, it still bears the stamp of the Anglo-Irish, and though I risk a literary martyrdom for saying so, their attitudes and personal presence are still evident in the city. Little can be understood about Dublin without some knowledge of this shrivelled breed.

Breed is not quite the right word. The Anglo-Irish are not a race. Indeed there is no such thing as a pure race in Ireland, where conquest, immigration, elopement and bastardy have, as elsewhere in the world, inextricably mixed the genes of its inhabitants. Irish patriots look back to Brian Boru as an Irish hero and regard his followers as the true Irish. And yet even they were the descendants of invaders. They were Gaelic-speaking Celts who had reached Ireland from the mainland of Europe only a century or so before Christ, displacing a small, dark race called the Firbolg, who have the best claim to be called the aboriginal inhabitants. And by the time of Brian Boru's victory, Norsemen had been settling among the Celts for two or three hundred years and in sufficient numbers to blur the racial distinctions. Successive waves of settlers from England made racial differences impossible to spot. Even the diehard Irish patriot, to whom Englishness is anathema, is likely to have English, Welsh, Scottish, Norse, German or Spanish blood flowing in his veins.

All the same, there are looks and physical characteristics that have come to be associated with the Anglo-Irish. Friedrich Engels, the social theorist and collaborator of Karl Marx, saw them as tall, strong and handsome, "with enormous moustaches under colossal Roman noses"; and it is an extraordinary thing that the looks of the Anglo-Irish often seem to match the more glowing descriptions of them. Yeats compared their women to gazelles, and I must court more Irish unpopularity by recording that once, at an essentially Anglo-Irish gathering, I was moved by the beauty, grace and grooming, the swan-necks and golden arms, the tigerish lethargy of long lank limbs, the dazzle of green eyes—and perhaps by the champagne—to think I was visiting Olympus. It was said of an 18th-Century beauty, a certain Miss Gunning, that the skin of her neck so much resembled the transparent white of alabaster that when she drank claret at official banquets the officers looked to see the red liquid flowing down her throat. That is the kind of physical attribute the Anglo-Irish have cornered for themselves.

In a city of many open-air markets, Moore Street (above) is known for its fresh fruit and vegetables—and for its aromas. A local comedian used to say: "Go down to Moore Street and get your nose educated." Market traders, such as the laughing cabbage seller on the right, still have the persuasive charm celebrated in the song about sweet Molly Malone, who sold "Cockles and mussels! alive, alive, Oh!"

The poet Yeats's infatuation with the Anglo-Irish, to whom he claimed to belong, was lifelong. "The greatest breed in Europe," he called them, and it is easy, by being selective, to sustain that illusion. Their natural good taste and delicacy of feeling became legendary: "Come into my garden," said the playwright Sheridan to a young lady, adding with characteristic grace and tact, "I want my roses to see you." They were noted for wit, a devotion to horses (Brendan Behan mischievously defined the Anglo-Irishman as "a Protestant with a horse" and I would add the horseman's bandy legs as another of their characteristics), amiable eccentricity and, during the mellow decline of their power, for living in damp, crumbling, ivy-coated and irresistibly appealing country houses, set among the lakes and trees of their overgrown parklands.

Their achievement was in fact more solid. They collectively lifted Dublin to its peaks of achievement. They created its shape and its beauty. They—not the Gaelic Irish—supplied almost all the greatest figures in Irish literature, art and architecture. The insular culture they forged in the 18th Century compares with those of the great ages in any country's history, and their brilliance was not confined to that century. Only a few years before Ireland achieved her independence, a small, mainly Anglo-Irish group collected around Yeats in what has come to be misleadingly called the Celtic Revival—a movement that occupies a towering position in 20th-Century literature.

There was a debit side to this account: the Protestant Ascendancy's official persecution of Catholics, lasting well into the 19th Century; the

A tinker sets out from his rolling home, parked near the Dublin Grand Canal. Like the gipsies of Europe, the tinkers live as a separate—and often despised—minority. They got their name from their traditional occupation as tinsmiths who moved from village to village mending pots and pans. Although most of Dublin's 200 or so tinker families still spend some time on the road, many have abandoned their horse-drawn caravans for cars and trailers, and they now tend to make their living as junk dealers or by taking odd jobs.

evictions by landlords of penniless, starving tenants and the frequent destruction of their hovels to prevent their return; the ruthless suppression of native Irish culture; the pervasive arrogance and conceit of the Anglo-Irish; and the often corrupt and brutal means by which they had come by their wealth. Yet the principal leaders of resistance to this oppression, and a long line of rebels and courageous dissidents, were in many cases Anglo-Irish too, providing antidotes to the injuries inflicted by their kinsmen.

After 1921, the Anglo-Irish were gradually ousted from, if they did not abandon, their positions of influence and power. But their presence has continued to be felt. Even today, though they do not parade their wealth or social qualities, many of them are there, on the boards of banks and insurance companies, defining the tone of some firms of solicitors, a few shops and clubs. Of these Anglo-Irish strongholds, the most resilient is the Kildare Street Club, where the landlords of Ireland still foregather to talk about horses and pheasant shoots. But Anglo-Irish or English accents, once hallmarks of the ruling class, can nowadays hinder a career in politics and many other vocations.

The Irish Irish have taken control of the state. They are not as cohesive a body as their predecessors, and they are likely to be confusing to the visitor. The Irish Establishment of today has a number of conspicuous shibboleths, chief among them the ancient Gaelic language, enshrined in the constitution since 1937 as the country's first official language. As such, the visitor expects to hear it on all sides. Instead he hears English, almost universally. He sees the curious script of Gaelic on buses and street signs, but if he asks passers-by to interpret them he meets, more often than not, with a blank stare. There are still Irish-speaking enclaves in a few remote parts of the country; and in some official Dublin circles—political, educational and bureaucratic—Gaelic continues to be written and spoken. But it has never experienced a thorough popular revival. The bus signs are the epitaph to a language; the English, in this respect at least, left an enduring legacy.

Not everyone would admit it. There are still people in Dublin who labour for the removal of all traces of English culture, and though they will never succeed, their existence explains not only those anomalous bus signs but a granite resistance to change in some official circles and a curiously xenophobic streak in priests, for instance, who fill their pastoral letters with warnings about the dangers of foreign dances and light summer dresses. The anti-English brigade are, in the main, the old generation of rebels whose young idealism has turned into crabbed hatred. They can be found now and again in the Dail, or parliament, and in the city's council, and in some church and Gaelic sports organizations. Here and there you recognize them in sombre suits, swathed in self-regard, their lapels festooned with emblems and medals that record their skills in Gaelic speech and sport. They have often been heard in the past urging censorship, proposing the destruction of old buildings that smacked too much of English styles, and exuding a general killjoy puritanism. But they do not obtrude so much on everyday life nowadays, and their influence is declining.

More obvious, more typical, and altogether more likeable is another type of Irishman: the archetypal Liffeysider, Dublinman rather than Dubliner, proudly distinct from the "conchies"—recent arrivals from the countryside. He is as hard a nut as the London cockney, with as adenoidal a voice. His conceit is impenetrable, and he lays down a law compounded of quackery, random fact, a smattering of religion, statute and medicine, and a refusal to be found ignorant of any subject. He is the man who holds forth loudly, like a preacher, in pubs, and writes self-confident letters to the papers. But his bark is worse than his bite. More than anything else he has been shaped by Dublin's ethic of live-and-let-live. Nearer peasant than prince, he is not refined. But he has a soft underbelly, a fund of good stories (if you can understand them) and a kindly concern for the stranger. Without him the work of the Irish Tourist Board would double, for more than other species of city-dweller, his is the image they project to the outside world.

There are, of course, other characteristic citizens: the new middle class, much like the middle class of other lands, but noticeable here as a novelty. (Twenty years ago, before Ireland entered Europe, attracted foreign investment, built up a modern industrial economy and graduated to affluence, they hardly seemed to exist.) There are, besides, the very poor and very rich, the smart young, the rebellious young and a great many other grades and shapes of Dubliner.

Nevertheless, there are features in most Dubliners that differences of age, wealth or cultural veneer cannot obscure. For all its bustle, there is still in Dublin a more sensitive awareness of people than I know elsewhere. When I arrive in the city, I am often surprised by the hallo's and thank you's, and that instinctive, wordless communication that other Western societies seem to have lost: looks exchanged at some droll happening, legs of the seated moving a shade more promptly for people to pass, whole sentiments expressed in the hunching of shoulders or raising of eyebrows.

There are other pervasive characteristics: gossip and litigiousness, a disarming capacity for hatred and grudges, and a huge, often endearing, national egotism whereby Irish products and Irish qualities put those of all other nations in the shade. Often in a Dubliner's conversation, the most exotic topics—the bronze gongs of Burma or the llamas of Peru—serve only as introduction to matters of purely local concern: Dublin's bell-ringing perhaps, or the zoological gardens in Phoenix Park.

Then there is the single-minded devotion to talk. If the spoken word, like energy, goes on and on, rises on wings to the sky, and forms ever-mounting clouds of verbal cumulus in the heavens, then a visitor from outer space would be led by his first encounter with this verbal stratosphere to think Ireland a far bigger country—and Dublin an infinitely bigger town —than either actually is. From old men and office girls, bars and bus-queues, the high-backed settles of Bewley's Oriental Coffee Houses and the open windows of suburban slums, prattle and banter, chatter and gossip, song and learned controversy float above the wide untidy streets, the steel-grey Liffey, the billboards and bunting, the orange, white and green of Ireland's capital, in a flow that only ceases—and then not entirely —for a few fleeting hours of the night.

Perhaps most disconcerting, Dubliners have a perverse love of the devious. "There is nothing like a knowledge of the Orient to prepare one for Ireland," wrote Honor Tracy, and went on to describe "the swimming sensation in the head, familiar to all who search for truth here". In a similar vein, Oliver St. John Gogarty, the Dublin surgeon, writer and boon companion of Yeats, described a friend as "one of those Irishmen to whom a direct question suggests the answer should be withheld". I realize, from encounters with many such, that my own lamentably literal mind will always debar me from feeling quite at home with the Dubliners.

Yet if I feel, as I confront these myriad dimensions of Dublin, like a man on quicksand confronting mirages, I know now to keep my nerve. I have learnt that in Dublin the opposite of a truth is another truth, not a false-hood. Time has blended my old romantic dreams and my newer, less favourable impressions. They are all true. So are the pocket Dublins of other visitors. That may be why most Dubliners (with the notable exception of the great writers) nod in apparent agreement at any two-bit theory offered by a callow newcomer. When from lack of a firm footing I am tempted to panic, I reassure myself that the ground underneath me will harden soon, and that behind every mirage is some existent fabric; that in Dublin, as nowhere else, illusion mingles with reality in an indissoluble alloy.

Old-Fashioned Charms

The spires of the church of St. John the Baptist (centre) and of Christ Church Cathedral (left) stand out against the sky as evening light dapples the Liffey.

Dublin is endowed with an abundance of assets, from the broad streets and quays laid out in the 18th Century to tree-shaded canals and ample parks—including the 27 acres of St. Stephen's Green in the city centre. Every shop, pub and doorway seems to bear the imprint of past generations, and Dubliners, in their loyalty to these familiar landmarks, have shown a decided aversion to change. Even the supermarket, so ubiquitous elsewhere in the West, has made comparatively slow progress against the local preference for small family shops with eccentric signs and oddly assorted wares. Time has tarnished the city, and the seediness of its slums is as striking as the sophisticated elegance of its Georgian architecture. But this very shabbiness confers its own kind of charm, which is why the inhabitants themselves often refer to their city as "dear, dirty Dublin".

Barely a ripple breaks the surface of the Liffey as it flows past Ormond Quay. The landing dates from the 1670s and was the first to be built on the north bank.

Accommodating a row of statuary, O'Connell Street—Dublin's main thoroughfare—leads past the columned façade of the General Post Office.

Tobacco, fruit and vegetables are among goods provided by a newsagent.

The franchise of a local post office extends to the sale of magazines.

Figures in formal attire decorate the window of a theatrical costumier.

A traditional butcher's shop makes obeisance to technological progress.

A moulded horse's head provides a stylish sign outside a saddler's shop.

Emblems of romance and good luck embellish the front of a jeweller's.

A barber's illuminated notice lures clients with a challenging question.

An umbrella held by a disembodied arm shows the way to a rainwear store.

A man paid to carry advertising posters through the streets finds the charms of a real-life girl more appealing than those of his two-dimensional companion.

The water level on this section of the Grand Canal is still regulated by well-preserved 18th-Century locks.

Caught in a sudden shower, people hurry across St. Stephen's Green, a park that was set aside in the 17th Century for citizens to "take the open aire".

Near the Grand Canal Docks, a Dubliner who has known better days idles at the corner of a partly demolished street that runs beside a derelict coal yard.

2

A Great Breeder of Extremes

Henrietta Street lies on the north side of the River Liffey, close to the city's centre. Its houses, built soon after 1720, are among the oldest in Dublin, and it is named after the wife of an 18th-Century English viceroy, the Duke of Grafton—a descendant, on the wrong side of the blanket, of England's Charles II. The street has other connections with society's upper orders. During the 18th Century, four successive archbishops of the established Protestant Church of Ireland were residents, and in the last decade of that century four peers and four members of the Irish parliament lived in its short, exclusive span. Horse-drawn carriages pulled up constantly to unload beaux and dandies, belles and shrewish old dowagers; and its drawing-rooms echoed to the kind of gilded bitchiness that the contemporary playwright Richard Brinsley Sheridan, born only one street away, reproduced in his *School for Scandal*.

Things are different now. Three adjoining houses in the street are reasonably well maintained as a convent, but most of the others are in an advanced state of decline. The efforts of conservationists have saved them from total decrepitude, but long ago their slender wooden staircases were replaced by unadorned concrete, their carved chimney-pieces sold at London auctions, and each of their floors adapted to accommodate three or four poor families. Windows are broken and patched; walls are whiskered with weeds; and gardens obliterated by tarmac. The homes of the aristocracy and gentry have become an unequivocal slum.

Henrietta Street, with its history of privilege and squalor, is Dublin in miniature; for this is a city that breeds extremes. There has been no time since the 18th Century when hunger, disease and deprivation did not crouch behind the sybaritic grandeur of the capital. The poles of want and surfeit, aligned with historic differences of class, racial origin and religion, have drawn apart the inhabitants of this city more noticeably and more persistently than of any other I know.

Those poles are not fixed points. Although rich and poor have been constants in the city's history, their whereabouts have not. The Dublin élite, who were once among the wealthiest and most fashion-conscious in Europe, were forever seeking to escape from smells and eyesores and from the risks of violence and disease associated with the Dublin poor, who were among the poorest. As a result, Dublin's development over the last three centuries has been rather like a fox-hunt, with the aristocracy and gentry for once becoming the prey and constantly striving to keep a safe distance between themselves and the deprived majority.

Evening sunlight strikes the gleaming white paintwork and mellow bricks of houses in Upper Fitzwilliam Street, one of Dublin's finest 18th-Century thoroughfares. The white window borders were designed specifically to reflect light and are a distinctive feature of the city's Georgian architecture, so-called because it developed during the successive reigns of the English Kings, George I, II and III.

The chase started out from the medieval city, on the high ground dominated by Christ Church Cathedral, where by the early 18th Century squalor and overcrowding had become acute. Developers with an eye to profit began to build smart terraces—rows of uniform and attached houses —on the other side of the Liffey in what is now the north-western section of the city, the area that includes Henrietta Street. The rich moved across the river, leaving the poor behind in the rat-infested lanes around the cathedral. More new terraces sprang up in the north-east, rising to the heights of Mountjoy Square, with its views across Dublin Bay and south-wards to the hills of Wicklow. Then, half-way through the 18th Century, a fashionable new district developed in the south-east, around Merrion Square and Fitzwilliam Square. Aristocrats, gentry and newly rich merchants began to move back across the river, and the north side of Dublin began to decline, although until about 1800 it still had exclusive enclaves like Henrietta Street.

During the 19th Century, north Dublin's fall from fashion accelerated, reaching the nadir around 1900, when the overcrowding, poverty, disease and depravity to be found there were said to exceed those of any town in Europe. Meanwhile, the Dublin élite continued to make good their escape to the south-east, moving out to the smug purlieus of Ballsbridge, Palmerston Park and Ailesbury Road. Recently the chase has been head-ing, slow and tired, through the suburbs along Dublin's south-east coastline.

The Liffey acts as a convenient divider nowadays, not only between north and south Dublin, but between rags and riches, slums and mansions, asphalt and greenery, working class and bourgeoisie, brashness and restraint. The division is not without exceptions. The pursuit of wealth by poverty has left eddies of residential distinction here and there, and not all the richest burghers fled in the same direction. There are quite exten-sive middle-class areas on the north side of the river, including the suburbs of Clontarf, Drumcondra and Sutton, while some of the peripheral housing estates built on the south side in the last 40 or so years by the city's authority—the Dublin Corporation—are pretty miser-able places to live. So, too, are parts of the Liberties, the area of run-down streets around St. Patrick's Cathedral.

But the north-south polarity remains, especially in the inner city. By and large, north Dubliners are more likely to need the crutch of the state for support, while south Dubliners are generally able to take care of themselves. Streets are usually wider on the north side—O'Connell Street is the widest in Europe—and they mostly intersect at right angles, whereas the layout of the south side is more intimate and curvilinear. Even the temperature in the wind-blown north is on average one or two degrees lower than in the south.

The south side seems mostly bespoke, genteel, tailor-made. While it fits well, it also constrains its occupants more. They live their lives mindful

The morning rush gets under way on O'Connell Bridge, the main span over the River Liffey. Built in 1880, the bridge is as wide as it is long—150 feet.

of the high standards of their dwellings. Their territory stretches from the quality stores of Grafton Street—Brown Thomas, with its arrays of smart clothes, Waterford glass and porcelain; and Switzers, where in living memory Madame Switzer herself sat among French furniture and prints, fresh flowers and the latest Parisian models, commanding young debutantes what to wear, how to hold themselves, how to behave—to the almost, but so perfectly not quite, uniform terraces of Merrion Square and Fitzwilliam Street. It includes the idyllic 27 acres of St. Stephen's Green and the Victorian neatness of Rathmines and Rathgar, districts farther south that have gone a little downhill since the days when British Army wives kept termagents' eyes on their households. It reaches out to the opulent suburb of Ballsbridge and the seaside villas of Dun Laoghaire and Dalkey. The people you notice, even if they no longer form the majority, tend to wear well-cut suits and stylish costumes, and their accents approximate more to English than to north Dublin. The trained ear can easily tell on which side of the river a Dubliner was born. Boots, for example, are "boots" on the south, but "bewits" on the north.

North Dublin, to the strict aesthete, is a disgrace. Like classic Irish greatcoats—bulky drapes of Donegal tweed that comprehensively protect against the weather—it serves a useful purpose for people with more important things than appearance to think, talk, worry, fight and sing about. It fits badly and hangs loosely; but its inhabitants seem neither to notice nor care. Their words flow, their consciousnesses stream, without regard to their physical setting.

It is a modern commonplace that, while the 20th Century is poor on pyramids, palaces and cathedrals, it cares for its old, young, sick, mad and maimed more solicitously than any age in history. Between them, the Dublin Corporation and the Catholic Church provide armies of social workers, welfare officials, priests, sociologists, nuns and psychiatrists to attend to the needs of the underprivileged. Officialdom is not callous. Yet its achievements in the north Dublin slums fall far short of its aims.

A visitor who walks along those once-distinguished terraces of Henrietta Street, Gardiner Street and Mountjoy Square in daytime is unlikely to see the worst violence and inhumanity of slum life. To him, the scene will evoke little more than a pungent nostalgia for days gone by. Lined old faces appear at decaying windows to look down on streets littered with blown paper scraps, on sons and daughters as they sit on doorsteps against a background of graffiti, while the grandchildren crawl or sprawl on the dirty pavements. Crop-haired teenage boys, with cubic shoulders and raised black shoes, swagger aggressively or utter simian mating-cries at passing girls—the unspeakable in pursuit of the unwooable. They seem to converse in a staccato of four-letter words, generative or excremental nouns and adjectives. They are a far cry from the novelists' picturesque Irish; but they offer little violence or direct abuse.

Night-time presents a different picture. The boys' courage rises, and their activities attract the police and the less timid social workers. Knives come out and gangs align. Society offers the young of this area neither work now nor any promise of work to come, for the nearby docks have been largely containerized and the building-supply yards that were once concentrated here have been moved outside the city. So society is reckoned a fair target for vandalism.

It is reckless to walk along the unlit no man's land behind Connolly Station alone, or through the neighbouring Sheriff and Foley Streets. An old woman of the slums remembered the time not too many years ago when there was "never a night a girl from these flats couldn't walk safe in from O'Connell Street. They left their own kind alone." Not now though. There are frequent rapes, robberies, muggings. Cars are stolen, stripped of saleable appliances, and sometimes set afire for final sport.

No class or category is free from mindless molestation. In a little settlement of houses for old people near the main bus station, vandals have variously tried to stone, firebomb and tunnel their way inside for no reason except to make life frightful. During the day a policeman stands guard for a period so that the inhabitants can go shopping and visiting. At another old people's home, children have been known to put flaming objects, fixed to wire coat-hangers, through the letterboxes of front doors.

There is nothing new in any of this except the technological hardware. Squalor, violence and human degradation are integral parts of the Dublin tradition. They date back—ironically—to the rapid development of Dublin in the 18th Century, when the plant of English colonization, after centuries of stunted growth, finally flowered in its full glory. Ireland reached a peak of prosperity as settler landlords or their sons or grandsons made farms more productive by new methods of agriculture. Exports of meat, dairy products and linen multiplied dramatically, and the capital grew rich on the profits of the countryside. In terms of status and population, Dublin became second only to London within what were then the British Isles. Just as the landlords of England had their town houses in London, the landlords of Ireland sported their newly built terraces and Palladian mansions in Dublin. Many of them appointed managers to run their rural estates and seldom visited the country, preferring the verve and good company of the expanding city.

The poor also flocked to the capital. They were driven by the new pressure on land created by a rapid increase in the country's population and aggravated by high rents for farm land and dwindling agricultural jobs. They were attracted by positions in service, urban building and trade. But Dublin expanded so fast—fourfold between 1700 and 1800—that there were nothing like enough jobs to go round. The slums were the inevitable result. Thus the 18th Century, which carried Dublin to the heights of its

Blocks of Dickensian tenements dominate the Liberties, the decaying area that lies between St. Patrick's Cathedral and the south bank of the River Liffey. The area derived its name from its status as the "liberty", or fiefdom, of the Cathedral, and lay outside the secular jurisdiction of the city until 1860.

social achievement and grace, simultaneously took it to the depths. The fact that most of the rural migrants brought with them their Catholic religion and the residue of traditional Gaelic culture, emphasized the economic divide. To the Anglo-Irish, secure in their Protestant superiority, the poor seemed a race apart, and were left to fester in alien squalor.

Throughout the 18th Century, visitors to Dublin commented with monotonous hyperbole on the poverty, disease and wretchedness to be observed in the city. The deformed, mutilated and diseased were everywhere on show, in worse condition, seasoned travellers agreed, than those of other European capitals. "Till I saw the beggars of Dublin," wrote the 18th-Century playwright Samuel Foote, "I could never imagine what the beggars of London did with their cast-off cloaths."

A detailed census of the city's population, carried out in 1798 by a Church of Ireland vicar, the Reverend James Whitelaw, and several assistants, revealed "degrees of filth, stench and darkness" inconceivable to anyone who had not entered the homes of the Dublin slum-dwellers. Statistics are the least compelling parts of Whitelaw's long reports. He described how, in the burning months of summer, he and his helpers explored "every room of these wretched habitations from the cellar to the garret, and on the spot ascertained the population". In the Liberties, "as I was usually out at very early hours on the survey I have frequently surprised from ten to sixteen persons, of all ages and sexes, in a room not fifteen feet square, stretched on a wad of filthy straw, swarming with vermin, and without any covering, save the wretched rags that constituted their wearing apparel. . . . Into the backyard of each house is flung from the windows of each apartment, the ordure and other filth of its numerous inhabitants; from which it is so seldom removed, that I have seen it nearly on a level with the windows of the first floor."

Whitelaw describes houses inundated with a wave of "putrid blood, alive with maggots" from an adjacent slaughterhouse. He speaks of whole families laid up with typhoid fever, of corpses decomposing in the streets, of collapsed walls and rotted floors, of landlords who continued to expect full rents, and in default of them removed such furniture as there was— blankets, doors even—and finally settled for eviction, never being at a loss to find new tenants. During frequent epidemics of typhus fever, patients were collected from their homes in carts, spilled out in front of the hospitals, and were lucky if the orderlies carried them in. In some parishes the cemeteries became so overcrowded that grave-digging involved the displacement of recently buried, still putrefying bodies, thus exposing the area and its inhabitants to noisome stenches and the serious risk of disease.

Even at the beginning of the 20th Century the slums were no better. Well over half the city's population of some 300,000 at that time lived in conditions that today would be considered grotesque for animals. Any number of reports and memoirs speak of the filth and bestial squalor of

Workmen installing a new gas main in one of the dingy streets of north Dublin carefully lay aside the old cobbles. At one time, cobbled roads were resurfaced with macadam, but pressure from conservationists has ensured that they are now restored to their original state.

the northern ghettos, commenting in particular on the overcrowding. Families tended to be very large, including not only a couple and their 10, 15, even 20 children, but often aunts and uncles as well. Such clans might occupy a single room, or two. A hundred people might live in one tenement house, depending for their water on a single tap in the backyard and sometimes using stairways and passages as lavatories.

With conditions of this sort persisting for at least two centuries, it was natural that Dublin slum life should acquire its own ethos, its own modes and manners and traditions, not all of them bad. In mitigation, there was an innate sense of community, fostered by the close packing of the population. Everyone knew his neighbours' doings and weaknesses, as well as their virtues; and the general ethic was a humane tolerance. The poor kept up a genuine comradeship and a humour heavily spiced with irony. Ballads were sung till late at night, and on summer evenings women swapped gossip from windows and doorways. Everybody had nicknames: "Juno", "the Paycock", "the Squib" and "the Dandy" are among those recorded in the plays of Sean O'Casey, which drew authentically on life in the northern slums.

The typical head of the slum household was addicted to drink, that temporary deliverer from human misery, and he usually made the lot of his family worse than it need have been. Novels about slum life—such as Paul Smith's *The Country Woman* and James Plunkett's *Strumpet City*— make much of the noble mother-figure struggling to keep her home and children decent and God-fearing, in spite of a bellicose, spendthrift husband who beats her regularly, rapes rather than makes love to her,

James Malton's watercolour of Capel Street looking towards the Royal Exchange captures the elegance of upper-class Dublin in the late 18th Century.

and in the morning presents a piteous, contrite figure until the pubs open and restore his self-respect. The picture is all too true.

In some ways, the ghetto-style degradation of the city was worse for the poor than the rural destitution they had come to Dublin to escape. All the same, Dublin offered what the country did not: a lottery of opportunity. Dublin was rich in patches, and there were various means of tapping the money into poor areas: begging, stealing and exploiting the weaknesses of the wealthy. The Anglo-Irish élite believed in the existence of a criminal class as if God had moulded the lower orders thus, and though no one nowadays would stop to argue about that long-disproved assumption, it is easy to see how it took root. Even the benevolent 18th-Century Dean of St. Patrick's, Jonathan Swift—cheered and greeted so often by the poor that he wryly claimed a yearly allowance of 40 shillings to replace the hats he wore out by raising them in acknowledgement—pointed out that poverty and cunning were twins. Beggars stuck to their rags, he wrote, "for their Rags are Part of their Tools with which they work". He considered most Dublin beggars "Thieves, Drunkards, Heathens and Whore-Mongers" and would have had them whipped back to their rustic provinces.

Prostitution was perennially high on the list of services provided by the poor for the rich, and bordellos were numerous at least as early as the 16th Century. By the turn of the 19th Century, Dublin's notoriety in this respect had spread far beyond the shores of Ireland. The trade in flesh was plied in open defiance of the Catholic Church, which had always been unrelenting in its attitude towards sexual misdeeds.

Gracious Georgian façades border the lush greenery of Merrion Square in south Dublin. "No city in Europe," wrote a 19th-Century historian, "is supplied with more extensive, more beautiful public squares, or so great a number of them, in proportion to its extent, as the city of Dublin."

Dublin's red-light district, known as Monto, lay on the north side of the city, between O'Connell Street and the Amiens Street Railway Station. Tyrone Street (now renamed Railway Street, to bury its associations) was the centre of it. "This side of the Yoshiwara," wrote the effusive surgeon Oliver St. John Gogarty, remembering it in his memoirs published in the 1930s, "there was never such a street as Tyrone Street for squalor with the wildest orgies mixed. . . . Here nothing but the English language was undefiled." The police tolerated Monto, as they did the fleshy merchandise of London's Soho, perhaps because it suited the requirements of the large English garrison of the day. In addition to the military clientele, aldermen, merchant seamen and various otherwise respectable citizens came here for whatever degree of pleasure they could afford. The area is much evoked by the franker Dublin writers. Gogarty lists and characterizes the madams of his time, and James Joyce in his novel *Ulysses* describes a comically perverse sado-masochistic scene in which Leopold Bloom is beaten and humiliated in a brothel run by Bella Cohen—a real-life figure.

Tyrone Street ascended east to west from the tawdry stews—where girls employed by Liverpool Kate, Piano Mary or May Oblong solicited passers-by, to whom they showed, by waving open their coats, that no time need be lost by undressing—to the luxurious premises of such as Mrs. Mack, Mrs. Hayes, Teasey Ward and Meg Arnot, which rivalled the best of Parisian brothels in the grooming of their girls and the elegance of surroundings.

Monto disappeared in slum clearance schemes and a wave of civil puritanism soon after Irish Independence in 1921. Dublin's former notoriety is diminished now, but a man walking from St. Stephen's Church in Mount Street to the Baggot Street Bridge on the Grand Canal can expect to be accosted several times by discreet ladies in fur wraps who emerge from the shadows. Massage is a euphemism for more indulgent practices in Dublin, as it is in London and elsewhere, and today there are male prostitutes as well as female.

The worst side of slum life in other eras—as now—was its enduring violence and anarchy. Like so much in the city, these were chiefly 18th-Century innovations. Dublin then was a dangerous place, with street robberies, housebreaking, looting of churches and shops, murders and child-kidnappings for money. Particularly in the first half of the 18th Century there were riots by the unemployed and running battles, sometimes lasting several days, between different gangs of workers and students. Huguenot weavers and their apprentices in the Liberties—collectively called Liberty Boys—were traditional enemies of the Catholic butchers, cattle-drivers and slaughterers in the meat-markets along Ormond Quay —the Ormond Boys. They clashed often. Their weapons were knives, stones and the cordoning of bridges that linked their territories. Almost always these battles brought casualties, sometimes deaths. Ormond Boys sometimes hung their victims on meathooks.

There were occasional arrests; but as often as not, the constables who arrived to make them went away injured. The Methodist evangelist Charles Wesley, on a mission in Dublin in 1747, watched as a constable was "beat, dragged about till they had killed him, and then hung him up in triumph. None was called in question for it".

To an extent, anarchy infected all classes of 18th-Century society. Ireland was then in the grip of a gold-rush ethic, with land, status, rural rents and titles in place of nuggets. If the poor were lawless, they took instruction from those rich who turned lawlessness into a code, who drank, fought, gambled, brawled, japed and duelled their way into folklore. Lord chancellors, chief justices, government ministers, dukes and earls settled their differences by "blazing"—duelling—in Phoenix Park, a dangerous place to stroll at first light; and, according to the anecdotal Judge Jonah Barrington, the questions asked by the bride's family about a prospective groom always included "Has he blazed?" requiring the answer yes if the suitor were to be regarded as a true man. Social position was granted by wealth as much as pedigree; titles could be acquired for money or, with a little delay, by tactical marriages. People were categorized by their incomes. "You are not invited to dinner to any private gentleman of £1,000 a year or less who does not give you seven *dishes* at one course, and Burgundy and Champagne," wrote Mrs. Delany, a cultivated socialite and friend of Swift, commenting on the gargantuan eating habits of the day.

It was an age—to some commentators at least—of bucks, rakes and dandies, of ostentatious spending and derring-do; and more than any other period, it clinched Dublin's reputation for eccentric recklessness. Freed from home law and the clamp of convention, English settlers competed with settled grandees in the arts of outrage. By day, beaux walked the path aptly called Beaux Walk in St. Stephen's Green, wearing cocked hats and canary coats, gold and silver lace, and tasselled boots

Georgian doorways in the St. Stephen's Green area of Dublin reflect a wide variety of tastes and styles. The principal decorative feature of such entrances is a semi-circular fanlight, or transom, filled with delicate lead tracery. So popular was this feature that it persisted into the middle of the 19th Century, long after Dublin's Georgian hey-day was over.

and violet gloves—mincing, flirting, inventing slanders as they went. By night, they took to their clubs and taverns—the Eagle on Cork Hill, Daly's in College Green—dissipating fortunes at the gaming tables, creating schoolboy shindigs, thinking up practical jokes, some of them on an epic scale. One memorable trick, for example, victimized the raffish Buck English (who once, having shot a waiter, had him charged to his bill at £50). English, a member of the minor gentry, had drunk himself into a stupor at Daly's. It was night-time, and his companions, on an inspiration, snuffed out all lamps and candles, closed the shutters and in pitch darkness continued to talk, laugh, shake dice and splash liquor into glasses. English came to his senses amid the din, and unable to see, imagined he was blind—as it was intended he should. The charade continued with the bandaging of his eyes and visits by mock doctors. He was reduced to a pulp of contrition for his past sins before they told him the truth. He soon went back to his old habits.

Some of these jaded dandies went further, dabbling with diabolism. A group known as the Hell Fire Club had their headquarters in a building on Montpelier Hill, south of the town. Here the first Earl of Rosse and his colleagues worshipped the Devil in black masses and—so the story goes—once burned a woman in a barrel. Another time they set fire to the building and remained drinking inside, for a foretaste of Hell itself. When Rosse lay on his deathbed in 1741, he received a letter from a pious cleric that catalogued his profligate ways and urged repentance. It was addressed simply "My Lord", without specifying his name. Rosse promptly had it re-addressed to the virtuous Earl of Kildare and expired happily amid a farce of misunderstanding.

Nastiness and brutality were interwoven with more picturesque idiocies, just as jungle law dovetailed or clashed with the administration of justice. The processes of law could be supplemented by bribery, the removal of witnesses or, as in the case of the Santry family, the threat to cut off

The sumptuous confection of fruit, foliage and musical instruments adorning the staircase ceiling of No. 20 Dominick Street (left) is the work of Robert West, Georgian Dublin's greatest master of decorative plasterwork. Particularly renowned for lifelike representations of birds, West included no fewer than 63 bird motifs in his embellishment of No. 86 St. Stephen's Green, including the fine example shown above.

Dublin's water-supply (which ran through their grounds) if their son was sentenced for a proven, gratuitous murder. The case was dropped.

Private justice was at times made to complement public justice, as another story, of a noble family, illustrates. Robert Rochfort, later first Earl of Belvedere, suspected after seven years of contented marriage that his wife had been unfaithful to him with his own brother. Her father, Viscount Molesworth, announced coolly that the accusation did not surprise him, his daughter having been born out of wedlock. Robert sued his brother for "criminal conversation" with his wife and was awarded damages of £20,000. When his brother could not pay, Robert had him committed to jail for life. For 30 years Robert continued to live sociably, building up a reputation for debauchery and generous entertaining. All this time he kept his wife confined in a country house. She was allowed to walk in the grounds only in the company of a footman, who tolled a bell to warn people away. When Robert died, she was released, gaunt, haggard, still wearing the fashions of 30 years before, and protesting her innocence.

Litigation became a national pastime and has remained so, owing to what a modern writer described as "the national love of a to-do and the national desire for revenge". Numerous cases in the 18th Century involved the rights of succession and inheritance, which were often tangled in a web of bastardy, bigamy, divorce and remarriage. One case, in which a deceased peer's brother tried to stifle his young nephew's claims to the title and lands of the earldom of Anglesey, dragged on for 17 years in mid-century, and was enlivened when the wicked uncle kidnapped, sold into West Indian servitude, and subsequently attempted to murder his rival. The issue was never satisfactorily resolved, since the Irish House of Lords found for one claimant, the English for another.

If all this crime, rowdiness and spunky bravado seems out of line with the quiet and tasteful cultural legacy of 18th-Century Dublin, it is because society worshipped two ideals. The names they gave these twin qualities were *ton*—literally "style" in French—and "bottom". Bottom was the gutsy side of life, a contempt for convention personified by swaggering squires, gambling dandies and men with mistresses. *Ton* was subtle and civilized, a matter of restraint, perception and fine distinctions. Bottom came from the belly, *ton* from mind and soul. Bottom was passion, *ton* was taste. The men who aimed their pistols at each other at dawn were the same who commissioned some of the finest architects, artists and craftsmen of the age. Girls who demurely concealed their blushes at fashionable balls were the same who flocked to be entertained by the public executions at Dublin's Newgate Prison and St. Stephen's Green. Mercifully, it is *ton* that has survived most noticeably.

The most impressive legacy of the Anglo-Irish is architecture. All the great landmarks—and many of the modest backdrops—that give Dublin its reputation for physical beauty and grandeur are the achievement of the Protestant Ascendancy. Two of the earliest are Trinity College and the Bank of Ireland. The Bank, begun in 1729 by Sir Edward Lovett Pearce, and added to during the next 70 years, witnessed some of the finest debates in Irish history when it served as the Houses of Parliament. Trinity College's library, edging a fine quadrangle on one side and a tree-lined sports field on the other, opened in 1732, a quiet giant of a building with what is still the world's biggest single-chamber repository of books. (Originally the building was girdled at ground-floor level by an open arcade with quoined arches, but these have since been closed in; nearby, barbaric new blocks shoulder up to the library like Mafia toughs.)

The construction of the florid, heavily domed Royal Exchange followed. Protestant churches were being built throughout the century, and new streets and squares enriched the contemporary speculators—the Gardiners, Dawsons, Molesworths, Fitzwilliams, Herberts—giving them a chance to immortalize themselves in street names. Not all the epitaphs have survived, since changing street names is a favourite and perplexing habit of Dublin's civic authorities. One early developer has fared moderately well because of his unusual approach. He called five thoroughfares respectively Henry, Moore, Earl, Of and Drogheda—his complete name and title. For inscrutable reasons, Of Lane later became Off Lane, and Drogheda Street was superseded in turn by Sackville and O'Connell; but the others remain.

Towards the end of the century, an English architect, James Gandon, was imported by Lord Charlemont, an embodiment of the Ascendancy virtues, a liberal statesman, patron of the arts, polished diplomat. Gandon was responsible for two of Dublin's most impressive buildings: the Custom House, where the business of the neighbouring docks was carried out, and Four Courts, headquarters of the judiciary, which stand in huge domed silhouette, like the eternal mother and father of the city. More fine buildings were to go up, but these represent the acme of Anglo-Irish achievement, a lovely amalgam of clean Palladian, busy baroque and disciplined neo-classical.

Among the attractive features of the Custom House are the curious, mannerist details of its ornamental capitals, by Edward Smyth, which represent the heads of the gods of Ireland's rivers: one has fish interlaced in his beard; another's hair is formed of scallops and mussels; a third has a basket of apples on his head. Detail is one of the delights of 18th-Century design; it ranges from such whimsical reliefs to the riot of rococo plaster-work—Venuses and Cupids, plants and animals and abstract patterns— that decorate the interiors of many of the period houses.

Against this background, and as remote as possible from the benighted Catholic poor, the social life of the Ascendancy went on: plays, assemblies and suppers to fill up the time. Dramatics—always a favourite entertain-ment among Dubliners, who can listen as well as they talk—throve in such

Mirrored here by the tranquil waters of the River Liffey, the Custom House is generally regarded as the most magnificent of Dublin's Georgian edifices. It was badly damaged during an IRA attack in 1921, but has since been meticulously restored to its former splendour, and continues in its modern role as local government offices.

theatres as Smock Alley and Crow Street. And actor-managers like Thomas Sheridan, father of Richard Brinsley, competed in signing up the finest actors from the London stage: David Garrick, Sarah Siddons and witty, lovely Peg Woffington. There were constant private theatricals too, in which the highest in the land, including Lord Chesterfield and other viceroys, sometimes participated. Dublin then had more concert halls than it does today; and in 1742 it enjoyed the most important musical occasion of its history. Handel, tired of London's fickle fashions, had come to Dublin at the invitation of the Viceroy, the Duke of Devonshire. During the first six weeks of a year's stay in the city, he composed *The Messiah* and the première of the world's best-loved oratorio was held at the Charitable Musical Society's Hall in Fishamble Street. Later, in England, King George II created a precedent by standing for the *Hallelujah Chorus*. There was no royal gesture in Dublin, but Mrs. Delany's parson husband was so moved by the pathos of the aria *He was despised* that he rose and cried loudly to the soloist, "Woman, for this, be all thy sins forgiven".

Less in the public eye were the activities of the city's learned institutions. Trinity College sent out a stream of distinguished scholars, politicians and writers: Swift, the philosopher Bishop Berkeley, the playwrights George Farquhar and William Congreve, the amiable, polymath poet, Oliver Goldsmith, and the writer and humane statesman Edmund Burke among many others. England herself could hardly match such a delivery of talents in their respective fields.

The Dublin Society—which later added "Royal" to the front of its name —was founded in 1731 to promote agriculture, manufactures and useful arts. Though famous now chiefly for its sponsorship of the Dublin Horse

Show, it has been one of the chief educational institutions in the country, researching and promoting new farming and industrial methods, raising standards of building, design and craftsmanship. With the more academic Royal Irish Academy—founded in 1785 to advance "Science, Polite Literature, and Antiquities"—these establishments formed the cultural backbone of Irish society.

The city's Catholics—certainly more than half the population by the end of the century—were allowed little part in the general progress. Some Catholics did well in trade, one of the few occupations they were allowed to pursue; but many successful merchants adopted the ways and attitudes of the upper classes and did nothing to heal the huge breach in society. Members of this renegade class were regarded with suspicion by the circles they moved among as much as by those they had left behind. They came to be known as Castle Catholics.

To Irishmen, the connotations of the word "castle" are different from those in other English-speaking countries. Dublin Castle was the viceroy's office, executive centre of English rule. During most of the 18th Century, the Irish parliament was its pawn, easily persuaded to ratify its decisions— the decisions of Englishmen. To the Castle's executive functions were added, throughout this period, the other trappings of a ruling élite. In its gilded, chandeliered state-rooms the rich and titled foregathered for levées, dances, dinners, concerts, the lord lieutenant's "drawing-rooms", or afternoon parties, and the annual St. Patrick's Ball—the glittering climax, held on the eve of St. Patrick's Day, of an intense six-week social season. Here debutantes curtsied to the viceroy before their acceptance into court circles; and here the viceroy, in granting knighthoods, touched the shoulders of kneeling worthies with the sword of state.

To the rest of the population the word castle had a more sinister ring. True, people assembled at the gates to watch the guests turn up in their finery and carriages. But they knew the Castle also as a garrison, a symbol —and sometimes more than that—of Britain's imperial power. It housed a secret service that used methods hallowed by time, if by no other authority, to extort truths about dissent. What the Bastille was to pre-revolutionary France, the Castle remained to many Dubliners until 1921.

Today the rich, in the old sense, are gone, swept aside by a rush of events of which Irish independence has been only one. The government has broken up the huge old estates. Aristocrats have no official place in Irish precedence. Those who remain can use their titles to good effect in certain circles—horsey and some financial ones in particular—but they are not numerous enough to count for much, and are subdued and tactful in their brushes with the populace. It would be a fool who would use the kind of language spoken by a Provost of Trinity, John Pentland Mahaffy, only 70 years ago, in disparaging one of Ireland's greatest writers: "James Joyce is a living argument in favour of my contention that it was a mistake to establish a separate university for the aborigines of this island—for the corner-boys who spit into the Liffey." (Joyce's opinion of Trinity was not high either: "The grey block . . . set heavily in the city's ignorance like a dull stone in a cumbrous ring.")

The rich today are not so rich as their predecessors. Nor are they distinguished by religion from the poor. They are an Irish class, grown up over the last 80 years. Brendan Behan, that swaggering Dublin playwright, himself of middle-class parentage, once described their ascent: "from stirabout and spuds, through porridge pots and hats and chatting about the servant problem, to *Angst* no less". Irish they are, but they are not above taking some tips from their Anglo-Irish predecessors. Certainly bows and curtseys have no place in their routines, nor does the Castle define the limits of their social ambitions. They are not landlords growing fat on the exertions of the rural poor. Their progress to affluence has been by way of the opportunities an egalitarian, consumer society of the 20th Century offers. No class barriers have blocked their paths. Castle patronage, once a substitute for merit, is a dead letter.

Yet they have their own systems of preference, based on any number of criteria: wealth, family, schools, societies, accomplishment in the Gaelic language or Gaelic sports (a boon for aspiring politicians)—even, in restricted but influential circles like commerce and banking, a certain Englishness of manner, accent and outlook. The breach that opened when mettlesome developers raised Dublin to the level of a cosmopolitan capital, and the country poor traipsed in for a chance of advancement, still gapes in spite of frequent patching. It takes no more today than a walk through the city, with all its contrary symptoms of want and plenty, to see that the extremes bred in that flurry of expansion have been perversely resilient offspring.

Aristocrats of the Turf

PHOTOGRAPHS BY LAURIE LEWIS

A pair of bowler-hatted judges contemplate entrants circling the ring during a Light-Weight Hunter Class event, while a similarly engrossed steward sits apart.

For six days in August each year, a showground in East Dublin becomes the focal point of the international equestrian world. The Dublin Horse Show—held on the premises of the Royal Dublin Society, an institution that promotes advances in animal husbandry, agriculture, and other fields—attracts more than 150,000 spectators. In the long programme of jumping and show events, nearly 2,000 horses compete in 88 different classes for trophies, medals and money prizes. As much a social as a sporting occasion, the Show brings together the remnants of the Anglo-Irish gentry, whose estate-owning ancestors helped set up the first Show more than a century ago. Secure on their home ground, these scions of Ireland's former ruling class provide a spectacle of poise and immaculate grooming equal to that of the thoroughbreds parading before them.

A smartly blazered owner gazes with proprietorial understanding at his elegant grey hunter, while one of the farriers employed by the Royal Dublin Society for the duration of the Show carries out essential repairs to a shoe.

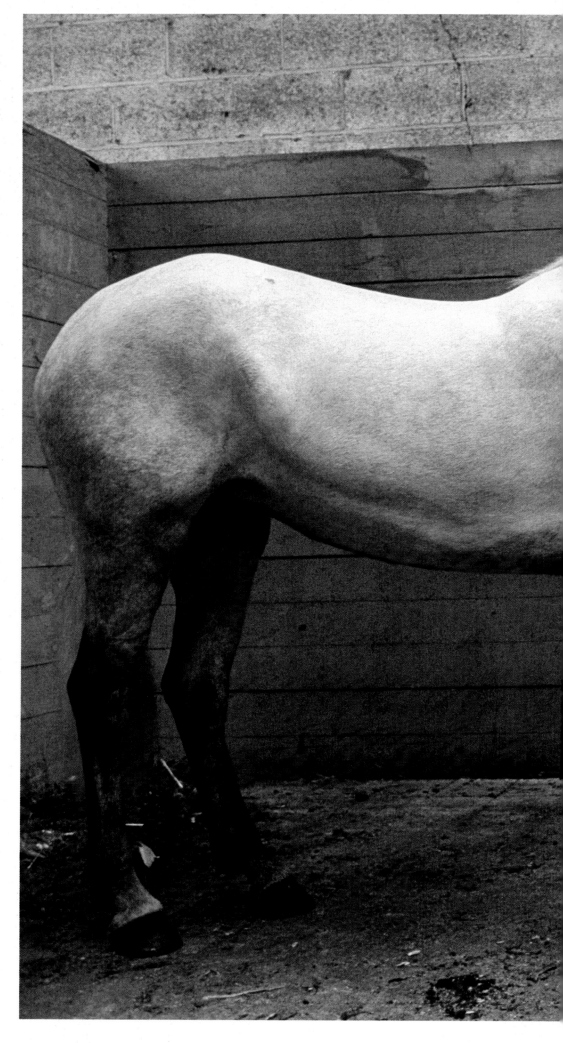

With a friend keeping her company before she takes her turn in the ring, a Ladies Hunting Class entrant, in obligatory hunting costume, surveys the competition.

After lunch on the first day, a well-dressed spectator, official catalogue ready in her hand, watches the judging of the Medium Weight Hunters in Ring One.

A stable girl holds one of the entrants in the Premium Mare Progeny Class, open to the offspring of prize-winning bloodstock from previous Dublin Horse Shows.

At the Show's half-way mark on the afternoon of the third day, the hounds of the Kildare Hunt prepare to lead a parade of prizewinners from earlier events.

Before the climactic international competition known as the Nation's Cup—a team of show-jumping event riders (above) study the terrain and pace out the distance between jumps. During the event, a member of the German team (right) gathers in his horse to clear the "treble", the sixth of the 14 fences in the competition.

On a balcony beneath a crowd of casually attired spectators, judges in formal dress line up for the presentation of the Nation's Cup at the end of the Show.

3

Rulers and Rebels

Easter Sunday in 1916 fell on April 23, which is the feast-day of St. George, England's patron saint, and the birthday of William Shakespeare, England's national poet. In Ireland, as usual, everybody went to celebrate Christ risen, but the day carried no more significance than in other years. Nor again did Easter Monday, although because it was a holiday people blessed the unbroken blue of the skies over Dublin.

There were clouds in the lives of some Dubliners, however. The war against Germany had killed or threatened to kill sons and husbands who had enlisted in the British Army. At home, two unofficial armies—the Irish Volunteers, a patriotic nationalist formation with 16,000 men, and the tiny Irish Citizen Army, a 200-strong but very militant offshoot of the Irish Transport and General Workers Union—were known to be stirring up trouble in the capital in the hope of freeing Ireland after more than seven centuries of British rule. Green republican uniforms (heather green for the Volunteers, dark green for the ICA) had been common in the streets for three or four years. Battle exercises had been held outside some of the most imposing, and—to republicans—most British, of Dublin's buildings, including the 18th-Century General Post Office standing in what was then Sackville Street and is now O'Connell Street.

But a holiday is a holiday. On that Easter Monday, people caught trams, or rode bicycles, or walked—and a wealthy few took their cars—to the sea, or Phoenix Park or the Wicklow Mountains, or the Fairyhouse Racecourse 10 miles away for the Irish Grand National, and others sat yarning on their doorsteps. Only a few Dubliners found reason to be in the city centre, but any who happened to pass near the General Post Office shortly before noon might have seen a ragged group of some 150 heavily armed men rush inside. Soon afterwards, two of the more smartly uniformed men appeared between the Ionic columns of the building's great classical portico and, as their comrades-in-arms assembled behind them and a small crowd gathered in front, one of them read a proclamation.

"Irishmen and Irishwomen," he began. "In the name of God and of the dead generations from which she receives her old tradition of nationhood, Ireland, through us, summons her children to her flag and strikes for her freedom." Passers-by continued walking, or if they did stop, seemed indifferent as the orator proclaimed the establishment of an Irish Republic as a sovereign independent state and announced the formation of a Provisional Government. When he had finished, his colleague turned and warmly shook his hand. If the crowd understood that a rebellion against

A bust of 19th-Century Ireland's greatest political leader, Charles Stewart Parnell, occupies the window-ledge of a cell in Dublin's Kilmainham Jail—now a memorial to past Irish rebels. Parnell was imprisoned here for seven months in 1881 after making violent speeches against the British government. But in his actions he was a constitutional reformer, unlike the hard-line republicans who were shortly to supersede him.

England was in progress, they showed no excitement. Wartime had inured them to curious happenings. They shrugged their shoulders, or smiled, or looked round expectantly for the police.

By now the sporadic sounds of shots could be heard everywhere in the city. Other strategic buildings were being seized, including the Four Courts, the Imperial Hotel, the College of Surgeons, Boland's Bakery and Jacob's Biscuit Factory. Dublin Castle, the seat of British government, had been attacked, though not taken. Yet there was no widespread sense of alarm. Shots were explained, as shots always were then, as target practice by the unofficial armies.

Some people paid dearly for their scepticism. At St. Stephen's Green, for example, bystanders saw youths running from behind the railings at the edge of the park, waving rifles and revolvers and commandeering cars and carts, which they wedged together to form barricades. According to one account, a cart-owner who remonstrated was abused and threatened, then given a count of four during which to walk away. By the fourth call he had not moved. He was shot in the head and killed. Despite this and other episodes that went far beyond the normal revolutionary high jinks, most Dubliners slept securely in their beds that night, a little annoyed perhaps, and a little disturbed by continuing gunfire, but confident that the British Army would soon put an end to the rumpus.

Despite the general indifference, these scattered outbreaks were the beginning of the most momentous event in Dublin's history, the Easter Rising. Sean O'Casey, at that time a member of the Irish Citizen Army and not yet known as a dramatist, was to describe 1916 as "the year one in Irish history and Irish life". Militarily, the Easter Rising was a disaster, but the events of the next few weeks led inexorably to the foundation of the Irish Free State five years later, and they still colour politics in Dublin.

The man who had read the proclamation on the step of the GPO was Patrick Pearse, 36 years old, a leading Irish Volunteer—and now President of the Provisional Government. His colleague was James Connolly, commander of the Irish Citizen Army and Commandant-General of all the rebel forces in Dublin. For many months, they and five other signatories of the proclamation had secretly been planning an uprising in Dublin. Connolly, a hard-headed champion of the Dublin working class, regarded the Rising as a way of achieving a social as well as a political revolution: capitalism would be overthrown, the ownership of Ireland would be vested in the people, and all differences of birth and privilege would be abolished. He was an exception. The other rebel leaders shared a very different outlook—romantic, quasi-religious and traditionalist. Several of them, including Pearse, were writers and poets.

Pearse, who sounded the keynote, was driven by a hatred for everything English and a love for everything Gaelic. He had been born in Dublin of an English father and an Irish mother, and had been learning Gaelic

At a meeting near Dublin in 1915 Patrick Pearse calls for recruits to the Irish Volunteers, the unofficial rebel army of which he was a leader. The Volunteers' professed aim was to ensure self-government for Ireland after the war with Germany, but Pearse and his colleagues had other plans. In 1916 they joined forces with the socialist James Connolly (below), commander of the Irish Citizen Army, and prepared to overthrow British rule by an armed insurrection.

since the age of 11 or 12. In his twenties, he set up his own bilingual school, called St. Enda's, and joined the Gaelic League, a cultural society founded in 1893 which encouraged Irishmen to throw off the "garbage" (as its first president, Douglas Hyde, called it) of English books, English manners, English games and the English language. This programme had a strong appeal for Pearse, who added a mystical nationalism of his own: "The Gael is not like other men. The spade, and the loom, and the sword are not for him. But a destiny more glorious than that of Rome, more glorious than that of Britain, awaits him: to become the saviour of idealism in modern intellectual and social life."

By the outbreak of the First World War, Pearse had become far more militant and was arguing that the only serious nationalism was armed revolt. Bloodshed came to dominate his thought. In his new, intransigent view, life sprang from death, and from the graves of patriot men and women sprang living nations. By his own and his colleagues' deaths, Pearse believed he would invigorate the spirit of Irish nationalism and make independence from England inevitable. Just as Christ had died on the Cross to expiate the sins of the world, so Pearse would die in Dublin to save the soul of the Irish nation. He explicitly wished to imitate the crucifixion, to walk to a new Calvary. "One man can free a people, as one Man redeemed the world," he wrote in a play called *The Singer*, making his hero MacDara speak for himself. "I will go into battle with bare hands. I will stand up before the Gall [Old Irish for a foreigner, in this case English] as Christ hung naked before men on the tree."

Had Pearse not been obsessed with the idea of a patriotic martyrdom, it is unlikely he would have ordered the rebels to march, for he knew that the Rising had no chance of success. Two days before it began, a vital consignment of arms from Germany had been lost. The delivery had been planned in Germany by Sir Roger Casement, an Anglo-Irish Protestant who in 1913 had retired from a long and distinguished career in the British Foreign Service and turned his energies to Irish rebellion. Because of poor communications between him and the conspirators in Ireland, the German steamer carrying the arms was intercepted by the Royal Navy off the coast of Kerry and was sunk by her captain to avoid capture. As a result of this failure, the Dublin insurgents went into battle without a single machine-gun, armed with rifles manufactured, for the most part, before 1870, and carrying even that traditional weapon of Irish insurrection, the pike. But that was not all. Since the plan of battle had been kept secret up to the last minute, and conflicting orders and rumours were flying all over the city, barely 1,500 rebels reported for duty. At the beginning of the rebellion they were outnumbered two or three to one by British troops, and the odds quickly lengthened against them. Risings had been planned to take place simultaneously all over Ireland, but few of any significance materialized, so the rebels had no safe hinterland to which they could retreat. Nor, because of their defensive positions, barricaded inside buildings, were they able to prevent the movement of British troops. All they could do was wait for the end.

It came, messily, in five days. After the first few incidents, fighting broke out between troops and snipers. Transport came to a halt, and petty criminals, or simply the very poor, took advantage of the confusion to loot Dublin shops, often wrecking or setting fire to them. Within 48 hours, as British troops poured into the city from elsewhere in Ireland and from England, the rebels were outnumbered 20 to one. From Tuesday evening onwards, the British employed artillery and incendiary shells to sweep barricades from the streets and bombard rebel-held buildings.

By Friday evening, the General Post Office was among the many buildings blazing in Dublin, and Pearse and his surviving comrades were forced out by the heat and fumes. Connolly, who had been wounded in the ankle earlier in the week, was carried out on a stretcher. Weak from exhaustion, the rebels took temporary refuge in some houses in Moore Street, around the corner; and on Saturday morning Pearse and Connolly decided to surrender unconditionally, signing a cease-fire order that was carried to the other rebel strongholds. By Sunday, April 30, the last of the rebel commanders had given themselves up, among them Eamon de Valera, future Prime Minister and President of an independent Ireland, who had been holding out at Boland's Bakery.

On Sunday, Dubliners were again able to move freely in the city, and they came out in large numbers to view the destruction. They found Sackville Street, which had been one of the most beautiful thoroughfares in Europe, a wreckage of gutted brickwork and smouldering heaps of rubble. In the city as a whole, 179 buildings had been destroyed. The streets were littered with masonry, half-burnt debris, cart-wheels and the shot-out remains of cars. The human cost had been 450 persons killed and 2,614 wounded, including army, rebel and civilian casualties. Most people were angry at the loss of life and property, and resentful of the rebels who had brought it upon them. "Shoot the traitors! Bayonet the bastards!" the crowds shouted as the main body of prisoners was marched away to army barracks that morning. Women in the poorest streets pelted them with rotten vegetables and emptied their chamber pots over them. So ended the military phase of the Easter Rising, as dismal a failure, it must have seemed, as the many Irish rebellions that had preceded it.

Severe and destructive though the fighting had been, the aftermath of the Rising left a far deeper and more lasting imprint on Ireland. The British authorities had already declared martial law on Easter Monday. Immediately after the cease-fire, they began a series of summary courts martial. Ninety people were initially sentenced to death. Although 75 of them—including Eamon de Valera—had their sentences commuted to penal servitude, 15 were executed by firing squad at Kilmainham Jail in the first two weeks of May. Pearse paid the supreme penalty on May 3. Connolly, who had been brought from hospital in an ambulance, was shot, on May 12, tied seated to a chair. A sixteenth rebel, Sir Roger Casement, who had been caught landing on the Irish coast from a German submarine, was hanged three months later in London, after conviction for treason at the Old Bailey.

Dublin, still shell-shocked by the Rising, hardly reacted to the first executions. But as penalty followed penalty, the mood of the city changed completely. The rebels, who had been seen as gangsters and even traitors, were transformed into martyrs; the forces of law and order were seen instead as agents of British colonialism; and the idea of an independent republic, which had been regarded by most people as an irrelevance and an illusion, gained a mass appeal among Irishmen. Pearse's vision of a blood sacrifice had come to pass, and it had achieved the desired effect.

Those who despair at the emotional and practical complexities of Irish politics would describe the Easter Rising, with some reason, as very Irish. That an event so Irish should take place in Dublin was somewhat unusual. For most of its history Dublin had remained loyal to the Crown, even when Ireland at large was shaken by sedition. To the Dubliner, violent rebellion was a disagreeable malaise that periodically infected the Irish countryside and the provincial towns. With few exceptions, only ripples of insurrection were felt in Dublin. And if a larger wave of civil disturbance lapped against this Anglo-Irish stronghold, it was as likely as not inspired by men who were more English than Irish. Occasionally an aristocratic ne'er-do-well flashed like a comet into the city's consciousness and burnt out with a bright flash and a dramatic suicide. Dublin Castle, the Bastille of Ireland, had been attacked more than once before 1916, but never stormed. For the most part, Dublin was the graveyard of revolutionary hopes, a place where rebel leaders met at secret addresses, and were betrayed by informers so efficient that the Castle authorities often knew more about a rebellion than many of its participants. And it was to Dublin that rebel prisoners were brought for trial.

But now, in 1916, after centuries of comparative calm, Dublin itself had been seized by the Irish revolutionary tradition. True, Dubliners had at first treated that tradition with a very English scepticism. Now, in nailing their colours to the revolutionary mast, they involved themselves, for good or ill, in the grand ideals and equally grand illusions of mainstream Irish history.

The vision of a land of free Gaels, so close to the heart of Patrick Pearse and the more romantic Irishmen of his day, was less than the truth. Ireland has never been a united, independent nation. She came nearest to it at the turn of the 10th and 11th Centuries, when most Irishmen spoke the same language—Gaelic—recognized the same Christian doctrine, and followed the same system of customary law; at the same time, Brian Boru held the High Kingship of Ireland almost undisputed and defeated a major Norse invasion in 1014. But already the coastal towns of Ireland were populated by the descendants of previous Norse colonists, and even during Brian Boru's hegemony, the Gaelic Irish were no more than a loose federation of small states led by kings who thought no further than their own interests, and would break their allegiance to the High King if they felt strong enough to do so.

Indeed, dissension among the Irish chiefs was the immediate cause of the Anglo-Norman invasion of 1169. Dermot MacMurrough—who had been King of Leinster, one of the four historic provinces of Ireland, but had lost his title in the chaotic tribal politics of the day—called in the Anglo-Normans as allies, and actually led this foreign expeditionary force across the Irish Sea. MacMurrough won back his kingdom, but the Anglo-Normans established a firm foothold and over the next few centuries became the leading power in the land. By the early 16th Century, a few families of Old English, as they came to be called, were ruling much of Ireland almost as their private fief.

But if Ireland was ruled in the main by Englishmen, it could not be said to be ruled from England. Settlers showed a strongly independent spirit. An almost chemical change in outlook seemed to affect all those who crossed the Irish Channel and made their homes in Ireland. The Irish way of life attracted them, and they developed an allegiance to Ireland that was the despair of the English at home. It was said of the Old English, in one of the most well-worn phrases in history, that they had become more Irish than the Irish themselves.

The most consistent opposition to English rule came, not from the Gaelic Irish, but from the Old English, particularly the FitzGerald family,

Painted 18th-Century ceiling panels dominate St. Patrick's Hall, the grandest state apartment in Dublin Castle, which for centuries was the seat of British government in Ireland. The hall, once the scene of magnificent balls held by the British viceroys, is now used by the Irish Republic for presidential inaugurations.

Earls of Kildare, who monopolized the powerful office of Lord Deputy, and were ready to rise against the Crown when their control was threatened. In 1534 they led a full-scale rebellion against Henry VIII, newly proclaimed head of the Church in England and, in the eyes of recalcitrant Irish Catholics, a heretic. They were actively encouraged by Spanish agents, who saw Catholic Ireland as the Achilles heel of Protestant England. This involvement by a continental power, which was to recur several times in the history of Irish insurrection, made a quick English response essential. Henry stamped out the rebellion and executed Thomas FitzGerald, son of the Earl of Kildare, who had laid siege to Dublin Castle. (Although their power was broken, the FitzGeralds remained important landowners until the First World War, when the head of the family, the seventh Duke of Leinster, lost the magnificent family seat of Carton, not far from Dublin, in a bet. He died in 1976 in a seaside boarding house in England.) Henry also gave up the feudal title Lord of Ireland, held up to then by English kings, and reinforced his authority by having himself declared King of Ireland.

Nevertheless, the difficulty of keeping control over Ireland was to increase rather than diminish, and relations between English rulers and Irish subjects became increasingly bitter. At the centre of the dispute was land. Whoever owned the land of Ireland controlled the country. The Tudors forced all Irish landowners, whether Old English or Gaelic, to surrender their estates to the Crown and then regranted them, thereby stressing that the landowners' only title now was through the king. The sole alternative was armed insurrection. During the reign of Elizabeth I, four major rebellions broke out in Ireland, and now the Gaelic Irish were involved. The most serious rebellion was the last, led by a Gaelic chief from the northern province of Ulster, Hugh O'Neill, Earl of Tyrone, and backed by Spanish troops. But at the battle of Kinsale in 1601, O'Neill was decisively beaten by Elizabeth's forces. Six years later, with his ally Rory O'Donnell, Earl of Tyrconnell, and over 90 of Ulster's leaders, he sailed for Spain, never to return. The event has been commemorated in the annals of Irish defeats as the Flight of the Earls. It marked the beginning of the end of Gaelic society, for without leaders, the Gaelic Irish were increasingly subject to the power of settlers.

Already before the battle of Kinsale, military repression had been reinforced by an insurance policy for the future loyalty of Ireland: the confiscation of land and its grant to settlers from Britain. In the idiom of the time, the land was said to have been "planted" with settlers. Now this plantation policy was intensified. The rebellious Ulster estates of Tyrone and Tyrconnell were systematically settled, in the main with Scots. The idea was to make the inhabitants of Ireland as British—and as Protestant —as the British themselves. Gradually the land of Ireland passed into the hands of the Protestant Ascendancy, and the mass of the Catholic Irish

A Dual Heritage

c. 200 B.C.	Celts, probably coming from France and the Iberian peninsula, invade Ireland
A.D. 432	The British missionary, St. Patrick, arrives in Ireland to convert the pagan population to Christianity
c. 837	Norse invaders found Dublin at mouth of River Liffey as a base for raids into Irish interior. The outpost begins to develop as a major port and trading centre
1014	Brian Boru, High King of Ireland, defeats the Norsemen at Clontarf, north of Dublin
1169	Anglo-Norman force invades Ireland
1171	Dublin falls to the Anglo-Normans. Henry II visits the city and grants it to colonists from Bristol
1172	Construction of Christ Church Cathedral started
1190	St. Patrick's Cathedral founded
1204-68	Dublin Castle completed as stronghold of English rule in Ireland
1541	Henry VIII takes the title "King of Ireland" without papal sanction
1601	Hugh O'Neill, Catholic Earl of Tyrone, backed by Spanish troops, attempts to halt English conquest of Ulster, but is defeated at Battle of Kinsale, near Cork
1607	O'Neill and his ally, Rory O'Donnell, the Earl of Tyrconnell—along with many Ulster chieftains— escape to the Continent in the so-called Flight of the Earls. Their lands are taken over by English and Scottish settlers, who begin to turn Ulster into a bastion of Protestantism
1649-52	After Irish Catholics support King Charles I in English Civil War, Oliver Cromwell subdues Ireland. Instead of receiving pay, his troops are given vast tracts of Irish land
1685	Catholic James II ascends English throne
1688	William of Orange, a Protestant prince from Holland, seizes the English throne and James II joins his Catholic followers in Ireland
1690	James II defeated by William of Orange at Battle of the Boyne, in the east of Ireland. William enters Dublin in triumph and attends a thanksgiving service at St. Patrick's Cathedral
1692	Catholics excluded from Irish parliament, which goes on to enact series of savage anti-Catholic measures known as the Penal Laws
1742	Handel's "Messiah" given first performance at the Charitable Musical Society's Hall in Dublin
1759	Arthur Guinness founds his brewery at St. James's Gate, Dublin
1782	Ireland is granted legislative independence, but British government uses its powers of patronage to control the Irish parliament
1798	Society of United Irishmen launch unsuccessful revolution. Theobald Wolfe Tone, their captured leader, commits suicide
1800	Irish parliament votes to dissolve itself and Ireland is incorporated into the new United Kingdom of Great Britain and Ireland
1803	Nationalists, led by Robert Emmet, attempt a coup in Dublin. The coup fails and Emmet and his co-conspirators are hanged
1823	Daniel O'Connell, a Catholic lawyer, leads campaign for Catholic rights
1829	British government yields to O'Connell's demands
1841	O'Connell becomes Lord Mayor of Dublin
1843	The British order O'Connell to cancel a mass meeting aimed at seeking restoration of the Irish parliament. O'Connell submits and the nationalist cause is severely weakened
1845-49	Potato blight destroys staple diet of Irish peasantry, causing disastrous famine. An estimated one million people die and an equivalent number emigrate, mainly to the United States
1858	Irish Republican Brotherhood formed. Its members, known as Fenians, dedicate themselves to freeing Ireland from British rule—by violent means, if necessary
1867	Fenians stage abortive risings in five Irish counties, including Dublin
1875	Charles Stewart Parnell, Irish Protestant landowner,

became tenant farmers with little security of tenure and living standards among the lowest in Europe. Every time rebellion broke out in Ireland, new confiscations and plantations followed. And with each new immigrant wave the racial stock of Ireland was modified, until Gaelic and Norse and English origins were obscured in a pottage of miscegenation, and the most evident dividing line became religion.

After the Tudor wars and the Flight of the Earls, Catholics still held two-thirds of the land of Ireland. Then came the Ulster Rising of 1641, which began as an attempt by the dispossessed of Ulster to recover their lost lands, and spread to the whole island, growing into an uprising of all Catholics to preserve their religion and defend their property and constitutional rights under the Protestant monarch. It was followed by 11 years of upheaval complicated by the English Civil War. After the execution of King Charles I at Whitehall in 1649, Oliver Cromwell, military commander of the Commonwealth of England, sailed across to Ireland with 3,000 troops to annihilate the remaining opposition, whether Catholic or Royalist.

Cromwell reached Dublin in the middle of August; but since the city had already opted for his side, his stay in the capital was brief. Incited by exaggerated reports of Catholic atrocities, he hurried on to conduct pogroms in Drogheda, Wexford and other cities, in which thousands of Catholics and Royalists were shot, knifed, piked, impaled, strangled and drowned, in deference to what Cromwell believed unwaveringly to be the will of God. The years of fighting had drastically reduced the Catholic population. Of the survivors, many thousands were sent as servants to the West Indies. A few hundred more were executed. The Cromwellian Act of Settlement of 1652 dispossessed the remaining Catholic landlords in Leinster, Munster and Ulster, and outlined plans to transplant them and their tenants to Connaught, the fourth and most barren of the Irish provinces, a composite of mountain, rock and bog. "To Hell or Connaught" was the puritan slogan for the despatch of papists, for whom either prospect must have seemed equally bleak. Many of Cromwell's own men received their arrears of pay in the form of confiscated land. Though the terms of the Act were not carried out with the ruthless thoroughness associated with Cromwell's name, the pattern of land ownership was transformed beyond recognition. More than any other single event, Cromwell's settlement sowed the seeds of 18th-Century Protestant dominance.

Catholic hopes rose briefly with the accession in 1685 of Catholic King James II, who installed a Catholic Lord Lieutenant in Dublin Castle; and after losing his English throne to William of Orange in 1688, he came over to join Irish Catholics in a rearguard campaign against Protestantism. On July 1, 1690, reinforced by 7,000 French troops sent by Louis XIV, he fought William of Orange at the historic Battle of the Boyne, near Drogheda, and lost. After this defeat, still celebrated every year by the Protestants of Northern Ireland, nearly a million acres of Catholic-owned

A Gaelic Motif

The medieval Irish harp has been Ireland's emblem ever since it first appeared on the coinage in the 16th Century, and the motif decorates buildings, monuments and sculptures throughout Dublin. Most of the images are based on a venerable instrument kept at Trinity College. Carved from willow and standing only two feet high, this harp was long thought to have belonged to Brian Boru, High King of 11th-Century Ireland, but is now believed to date from the 14th Century. Such harps had been played in Ireland since pre-Christian times, and Gaelic harpers who performed at feasts or accompanied the early Celtic bards were renowned for their skill throughout Europe.

Nowadays, no figure of Hibernia—a female personification of Ireland, not unlike England's Britannia—is complete without her harp, as various illustrations on these pages confirm. She holds one on top of the Custom House (top row, left) and on top of the General Post Office (top row, centre); over the entrance of the Royal Dublin Society (centre row, second from left) and in a stained-glass window of a building belonging to the Society (bottom row, second from right). A harp standing on its own is also a common motif—seen, for example, on a bronze plaque at City Hall (top row, second from left) and on the side of a brewer's delivery truck (top row, second from right).

In the Genealogical Museum at Dublin Castle, Irish harps are joined with English lions in a coat of arms (top row, right) dated 1783 and inscribed with the confident Latin motto *Quis separabit*, or "Who shall separate them?" In a more characteristic association, a golden harp decorates the monument in O'Connell Street to that champion of Irish self-government, Charles Stewart Parnell (centre row, right), reminding onlookers that the Gaelic tradition is an inseparable part of Ireland's national consciousness.

land were confiscated, and Catholic landholdings in Ireland fell from about a quarter to one-seventh.

Over the next 30 years, the victorious Protestants in the Dublin parliament attempted to avert the threat of further Catholic insurrection by passing several packets of Draconian legislation that came to be known as the Penal Laws. Penal they were. Catholics were forbidden to sit in the chamber or vote in parliamentary elections, to join the bar or the bench, to attend Ireland's one university (Trinity College, Dublin), to serve in the navy or any public bodies, to run a school, bear arms, marry a Protestant, buy, inherit or in any other way receive land, or own a horse worth more than five pounds. It was even proposed, though not enacted, that Catholic priests should be castrated. By the Penal Laws the vast majority of the Irish people were given an inferior status. Recognizing the magnitude of their defeat, more than 10,000 Irish troops who had fought for James II sailed away into exile on the Continent, many to fight against England in the armies of France and Spain. It was an exodus as final and as symbolic as the Flight of the Earls a century before, and it is commemorated in Ireland as the Flight of the Wild Geese.

The 18th Century became the golden age of Irish Protestantism. But it was not, from England's point of view, a greatly less troublesome period. The persistent tendency of Ireland to drift out of English control reasserted itself again. The Anglo-Irish of the Protestant Ascendancy, although distinct from the native population, had no more wish than their Old English predecessors to toe the English line. Like the contemporary English colonists in America, they found that England was a demanding parent. She insisted on legislating for Ireland, on prohibiting certain trades and manufactures that conflicted with her own interests, and on raising taxes for her exclusive benefit. Now that the Anglo-Irish had consolidated their power and entrenched themselves against foreseeable Catholic dangers, they saw less and less reason to pay a protection fee of money and subservience, and applied increasing pressure to break their dependence.

In the first half of the century one of the most vitriolic exponents of Anglo-Irish resistance was Jonathan Swift, Dean of St. Patrick's Cathedral in Dublin, whose loathing of English interference was the greater because he had failed, not without efforts, to make a mark in English politics. His wit was caustic. "Burn everything English except her coal," he urged his fellow citizens. In a sustained and savage piece of irony, directed against the economic restrictions that reduced so many Irish to penury, he proposed that the problem of the superfluous children of the poor could be solved by slaughtering and preparing them for the tables of the rich. His essay goes so far as to recommend recipes for this tender meat. He also lampooned the Protestant bishops sent over from England by suggesting that they were imposters; the real clergy, he explained—worthy men all—

Carved in stone, a member of the defunct Dublin Metropolitan Police—founded in the 1830s and bitterly resented by Irish nationalists —still decorates the outside of a police station in the capital. The force was disbanded in 1922 and replaced by the Civic Guard, the police of the new Irish Free State.

had been waylaid and murdered *en route* by highwaymen, who had disguised themselves in their victims' clothes and come over to take up their well-paid positions.

Towards the end of the 18th Century, opposition to England grew among the Protestant landowners who sat as MPs for Ireland in the magnificent new parliament building on College Green. With their parks, coverts, Palladian mansions and productive farms in the country, and their terraced houses on the spacious streets and squares of the capital, they were grandly self-confident, and they produced heroes of their own who found honoured places in the Irish pantheon. In the 1770s Henry Grattan, a Dublin lawyer and parliamentarian, won growing support for independence by his brilliant oratory. "Nations," he declaimed, "are governed not by interest only, but by passion also, and the passion of Ireland is freedom." In 1782, inspired by the example of the American Declaration of Independence, Grattan persuaded the Dublin parliament to pass an Irish declaration of legislative independence. The following year the British government in London, anxious not to have an Irish as well as an American revolution on its hands, passed an Act of Renunciation in parliament at Westminster that affirmed the exclusive right of the Dublin parliament to legislate for the Irish people. For the first time in history, Dublin was a capital in the full sense of the word. But the spirit of optimism that followed the Act of Renunciation was to be short-lived.

In theory there were now two independent kingdoms, one British and one Irish, under a common Crown. In practice, though, the British government still controlled Ireland, because it continued to nominate the viceroy and chief secretary at Dublin Castle, who were the executive arm of Irish government. What sounded like independence was in fact a sham. Moreover, the vast mass of the Irish people—Catholics and poor Protestants—were without political influence.

Even this nominal independence of what Grattan called the "Protestant nation" of Ireland was seen by conservative forces in England as an excessive concession, the beginning of a surrender that might end in the creation of a Catholic state closely bound by spiritual ties to England's main continental enemy, France. Their fears intensified in 1789 when the storming of the Bastille signalled the greatest political upheaval of the 18th and 19th Centuries: the French Revolution. Nor were they alone in their concern. The revolutionary ideals of liberty and equality posed as much of a threat to the Anglo-Irish minority as it did to other élites, and Protestants who, ten years before, had campaigned for autonomy from England now began to look once again for the reassurances of the English connection.

The revolutionary threat was most eloquently enshrined in the speeches and writings of one of their own number, Theobald Wolfe Tone, a middle-class Dublin Protestant, descended from a Cromwellian soldier

Statues of Queen Victoria, allegorical figures and a British commissioner of education languish in the quadrangle of Kilmainham Royal Hospital, which awaits conversion to a museum or arts centre.

and educated at Trinity College. Tone was the first man to talk per-
suasively of an Ireland controlled by Irishmen, regardless of their race or
religion. His vision came to be regarded as prophetic by the rebels of 1916,
not only for its content but because Tone, as one of the master-minds in
the Society of United Irishmen—an organization dedicated to an independent republic of Ireland—was to play a daring and ultimately tragic part
in the abortive revolution of 1798. His statement of aims, recalled by
Patrick Pearse at the annual commemoration over Tone's grave in 1913,
is a sacred text among Irish republicans. "To break the connection with
England, the never-failing source of all our political evils, and to assert the
independence of my country—these were my objects. To unite the whole
people of Ireland, to abolish the memory of all past dissensions, and to
substitute the common name of Irishman in place of the denominations of
Protestant, Catholic and Dissenter—these were my means."

During the 1790s, the political temperature of Ireland rose year by
year. Agrarian violence was on the increase. Bands of men roamed the
countryside at night, destroying property, killing cattle and murdering
anyone who stood in their way. In the cities, middle-class radicals like
Tone met to plot and subvert. Belfast, in those days largely reformist and
republican, was the northern capital of the United Irishmen, and Dublin
the southern capital. Tone, a chronic optimist, saw hopeful signs everywhere. He was heartened that Dubliners were beginning to address each
other as "Citizen", in the French fashion. In Back Lane, close to Christ
Church Cathedral, he sat with the Catholic Committee and helped them
campaign for the repeal of the Penal Laws at a time when Protestants, in
the words of Christine Longford, in her book on Dublin, "thought that
Catholics had horns and hoofs".

The English, acting through the pliable government at Dublin Castle
and aware that war with France was imminent, attempted both to placate
and to control the Irish with alternate concessions and repression. Several
rights that had been denied to Catholics under the Penal Laws were
restored—including, in 1793, the freedom to vote in parliamentary
elections. But in 1796, after the efficient network of spies working for the
Castle had reported that the United Irishmen were planning open
revolt with French backing, the government suspended habeas corpus,
strengthened the militia and carried out systematic searches for arms in
town and country. For two years, these policies forestalled a number of
Irish conspiracies and brought in some notable prisoners, including the
Duke of Leinster's son Lord Edward FitzGerald, a romantic and amiable
young man who, like Tone, had abandoned the cause of his class for the
democratic hopes of the United Irishmen. In March 1798, Lord Edward
was surprised by police at a meeting of the United Irishmen in Bridge
Street, a stone's throw from the Liffey. He escaped and hid for two
months, but was finally discovered and arrested after a scuffle in which he

In an artist's reconstruction of a notorious double attack on British authority in 1882, Lord Frederick Cavendish, Chief Secretary of Ireland, faces four stiletto-wielding assassins just before being stabbed to death in Phoenix Park, Dublin. The men, members of a rebel group called The Invincibles, had already killed the Under-Secretary, T. H. Burke, whose body lies in the background.

was mortally wounded. In spite of such harassment, the 1798 Uprising broke out a few days later, at the end of May.

It was doomed before it began. Over a period of eight weeks, there were unco-ordinated risings in various parts of the country, all of them quickly suppressed, but several with appalling loss of life. Dublin remained firmly under British control. The Castle was barricaded and defended by gunners with burning tapers at the ready. The city lamp-lighters were kept at their work, as the Bishop of Dromore recounted in a letter, with "a bayonet in the breech". Then, long after they could have been useful, the French arrived. One ship unloaded the main body of troops on the west coast in August; a further, unsuccessful attempt to land troops was made in September and another in October. Each invasion ended in retreat or capitulation—and the prisoners included Wolfe Tone, who had spent the last two years in Paris enlisting French aid. He was taken through Dublin, fettered and on horseback. At his court martial, though he pleaded for a soldier's death by shooting, he was sentenced to hang for treason. When, in his prison cell, he learned that the gallows were being prepared, he cut his throat with a razor.

The failure of the 1798 Uprising dashed the hope of the conspirators that Irishmen might unite for an Irish cause. A militia manned almost entirely by Irish recruits had carried out most of the government's military actions. Irish nationalist had fought against Irish loyalist, Protestant against Catholic, and tenant against landlord. It had been less a fight for freedom than an Irish civil war, and across the country 30,000 Irish lives had been lost.

Shaken by what to many Englishmen seemed the consequence of a taste of freedom, England acted decisively. William Pitt, then British prime minister, called a halt to Irish self-government by pushing through the Act of Union in 1800. Under the terms of this legislation, Ireland was swallowed up in the United Kingdom of Great Britain and Ireland. Dublin, from being capital of a country at least nominally independent, was demoted to a provincial town. The fine parliament building was converted into a bank, which it has remained ever since, and Dublin's most elegant era came to an end. Many Anglo-Irish peers abandoned Dublin and became absentee landlords running their Irish estates from England. The aspirations of the Anglo-Irish were irretrievably buried. In their place came the aspirations of the Catholic Irish, whose resistance to the British connection increased during the 19th Century and led, though not inevitably, to the Easter Rising of 1916.

Dubliners had been shown a choice between moderation and extremism in politics, between the kind of constitutional reform under the British Crown urged by Grattan, and the violent republican revolution preached and practised by Tone. During the 1798 Uprising they had come down firmly on the side of law and order, and during the 19th Century they put their trust in constitutional reform. But the policy of violence was not extinct. In 1803 there was a brief flash of rebellion in Dublin when another Protestant idealist, Robert Emmet, younger brother of one of the United Irishmen, made a new and hopeless attempt to set up an independent Irish republic. His rising was no more than a romantic gesture, but Tone's example continued to inspire generations of republicans who, for the most part, were content to wait for their moment in the wings of history.

The greatest leaders of the Irish during the 19th Century were not revolutionaries. Neither Daniel O'Connell, in the first half of the century, nor Charles Stewart Parnell, in the second, issued a call to arms. They envisaged an Ireland in the hands of the Irish but governed by English-style institutions and, like Grattan's Ireland, remaining within the framework of the British Empire. They differed from the Anglo-Irish of Grattan's day in campaigning for the rights of Catholics as well as Protestants, and from their successors of the 20th Century in not insisting on total severance from England.

Their achievements were massive. Early in the 19th Century, Irish Catholics still did not have the right to sit in parliament (which after 1800 meant the Westminster parliament, where Ireland was represented by some 100 MPs). Catholic Emancipation, or the regaining of that parliamentary right, became the battle-cry of Daniel O'Connell, a leader of immense energy and resourcefulness. He created the first mass constitutional reform movement in Ireland, and in 1829 succeeded in getting an Act for Catholic Emancipation passed at Westminster. His next campaign was for repeal of the Act of Union, and the consequent restoration of self-government. To this the British government remained resolutely opposed, and in 1843 ordered him to cancel a mass meeting planned at Clontarf on the outskirts of Dublin, where Brian Boru had defeated the Norsemen. O'Connell acquiesced. Within five years both he and his repeal movement were dead.

Before a new initiative towards Irish self-government could be taken, a historical catastrophe of the first magnitude intervened. Between the late 18th Century and the early 1840s, the population of Ireland had grown from about four million to more than eight million. Because of the traditional Irish system of inheritance, the land available for peasant cultivation had been divided and sub-divided until most tenant farmers lived on tiny smallholdings, many of them growing potatoes as their only crop. Disaster struck first in 1845, and every year thereafter until 1849; in each of those years crops were ruined by *Phytophthera infestans*, commonly known as potato blight, which reduces potatoes to stinking slime. As many as one million Irish people died of famine and disease. Another million emigrated, chiefly to the United States, where their resentment of the English and a willingness to fund Irish rebels took lasting root. Emigration became established as an escape from poverty and a stagnant

Nelson's Column in O'Connell Street (left), erected in 1808 to commemorate the victorious admiral of the Battle of Trafalgar, long symbolized British power in Ireland. But one night in March, 1966—50 years after the Easter Rising—a bomb blast reduced it to a stump (below), and it has since been replaced by an island of cobble-stones and flower-beds.

society. By the end of the 19th Century the population of Ireland had fallen once more to only four and a half million, and it was to continue dropping until 1961, when it reached less than four and a quarter million.

The Great Famine left a legacy of bitterness and hatred against the British, who were blamed for not providing sufficient relief, and it lastingly tainted relations between the two countries. Nevertheless, most Dubliners, like most other Irishmen, were ready to accept reform rather than revolution. Under the leadership of Charles Stewart Parnell, they continued to campaign not for separation but for Home Rule and the transfer of farmlands to the tenants who worked them. By the beginning of the 20th Century, that objective had been largely achieved through sympathetic British legislation. Home Rule might well have been attained also, had it not been for a personal scandal that ended the career of Parnell when he was at the height of his influence.

Parnell was a Protestant and a landowner. By the brilliance of his political tactics he became the uncrowned king of Ireland, the leader of Protestants and Catholics alike. "We cannot look upon a single Irishman as not belonging to us," he said; and in response Dublin went Parnellite. When Parnell was not at Westminster, holding the balance in the House of Commons with his following of Irish MPs, he was given a hero's welcome in Dublin. In 1881, when he was imprisoned at Kilmainham Jail on suspicion of encouraging agrarian unrest, there were riots in the city. Ladies sent him green smoking caps, green tea cosies, green socks and a green satin quilt. Agrarian unrest, rather than diminishing, increased. Parnell was soon released by the British.

Parnell's gift was an ability to contain the revolutionary potential of Ireland. Since the collapse of Daniel O'Connell's repeal movement in 1843, a secret society dedicated to violent rebellion had emerged. This was the Irish Republican Brotherhood, whose members were generally known as Fenians, from the name of an ancient Irish military caste. They were responsible for an abortive rising in Ireland in 1867, coupled with raids into England, including a bombing at Clerkenwell in London that killed 20 people. In 1882 another group called the Invincibles attacked the British chief secretary and under-secretary outside the Viceregal Lodge in Phoenix Park and stabbed them to death. Parnell was so obviously shocked by the murder that his reputation survived untarnished. William Gladstone, three times British Prime Minister, was confident in Parnell and an earnest believer in Home Rule himself. Though the English House of Lords would be a stumbling-block for the passage of a bill through parliament, Home Rule for Ireland was nevertheless an attainable objective. But scandal intervened.

For some time, Parnell had been living secretly with a married woman, Kitty O'Shea, and she had had two children by him. In 1890, this liaison became public. Mrs. O'Shea's husband, possibly prompted by British opponents of Home Rule, cited Parnell as co-respondent in divorce proceedings. Parnell, leader of Europe's most rigidly Catholic society, was ruined, and within a year he was dead.

In spite of the abuse and recriminations directed at him during his final months, and of signs of a belated conversion to the politics of violence, he was given an impressive Dublin funeral. The coffin ("The box that held all Ireland had," Sean O'Casey called it) was carried head-high in the rain from the Westland Row Station, where it had arrived from England, to Glasnevin cemetery, where it was set to rest in a vault close to other heroes of the nation.

After Parnell, the Home Rule party at Westminster, though split into warring factions, continued to campaign under new leaders, chiefly John Redmond, and by 1914 had actually succeeded in getting a Home Rule bill through parliament, though the measure was not to take effect until after the First World War. Nevertheless Redmond lacked Parnell's lustre and prestige, and the delay in granting Home Rule played into the hands of forces dedicated to the narrower concept of a Gaelic Ireland, and to the violent overthrow of British government. The Gaelic movement, based in Dublin, provided a core of sentiment for the independence movement. The Irish Republican Brotherhood, which by the start of the war counted Patrick Pearse and most of the other signatories of the 1916 proclamation among its members, supplied the revolutionary impetus. England's pre-occupation with the European war gave the opportunity, and the short, decisive drama of spring 1916 was acted out with all its bloodshed and savage retribution.

In the opening years of the 20th Century, a new party called Sinn Fein (Ourselves Alone) had been formed, denying the right of the English parliament to govern Ireland, and dedicated to the attainment of national self-government under the English Crown. In the wake of the Easter Rising, Dubliners and the majority of Irishmen turned their backs on the old Home Rule party and in the 1918 General Election voted for Sinn Fein, which by then had adopted an out-and-out policy of cutting all links with Britain. Conventional political means had been discredited, and although Sinn Fein was ostensibly against violence, its connections with militant leaders ensured that violence would soon be enshrined as the first principle of an independent Ireland.

Unwilling to take up their seats at Westminster, the victors in the 1918 election set up a Dail Eireann, or Irish parliament, in the Mansion House in Dublin in 1919. The 1916 proclamation of independence was read again, and Eamon de Valera, the only surviving officer of the Easter Rising, was elected president. De Valera was a curiously ascetic figure, stern and un-compromising, and far from being a master of either rhetoric or logic. Yet he was to dominate Irish politics for half a century and to become the only

In Glasnevin cemetery, a wreath with orange, white and green ribbons—the colours of the Irish Republic—decorates a family grave containing the body of Eamon de Valera, modern Ireland's most prominent politician. A rebel commander during the Easter Rising, he was three times Prime Minister and finally President of the Republic until 1973.

politician of this infant state to gain anything like world stature.

The Irish Volunteers changed their name to the Irish Republican Army and launched a guerrilla war on the British Army and police. In response, the British raised the number of their troops in Ireland to more than 40,000, including a body of war veterans and rough elements nicknamed the Black and Tans, after the colour of their uniforms. The rising that Pearse and Connolly and their colleagues had dreamed of in 1916 now occurred in earnest. For two years the struggle continued, with the loss of some 1,300 lives and the destruction of property in many parts of the country including Dublin, where the Custom House was fired by the IRA on the grounds that it was an enemy installation. The British Prime Minister, David Lloyd George, sought a solution that would satisfy the demand for Irish independence and at the same time prevent a new civil war erupting in the north, where the Protestants had been training their own Ulster Volunteers since 1913 and were ready to fight rather than join a papist Ireland.

In 1921, Lloyd George invited de Valera to negotiate a treaty, and five plenipotentiaries, led by the prominent Sinn Feiners Arthur Griffith and Michael Collins, were sent to London to hammer out terms. The treaty they signed, after prolonged discussions, established the 26 counties of southern Ireland as the Irish Free State, a self-governing Dominion within the British Empire. The members of the new parliament were to take the oath of allegiance to the British Crown. The six most heavily Protestant counties of the north, which had been given their own parliament the previous year, were left the option of joining the Dominion or remaining part of the United Kingdom, although their choice was a foregone conclusion.

Confusion broke out in Dublin when the terms were announced. De Valera and two others in his cabinet refused to accept the treaty, chiefly over the issue of the oath of allegiance. The Dail passed it, de Valera resigned, and Arthur Griffith became president of a provisional government, pending a general election to ratify the new constitution. Dublin Castle, the Viceregal Lodge and the barracks, which for 700 years had been the centres of British rule, were handed over to the new state. But the momentum of Irish rebellion was impossible to stop. The minority who opposed the treaty embraced violence and again launched the campaign for an independent republic. During the next few months, in an atmosphere of growing disorder, recalcitrant republicans barricaded themselves inside the Four Courts building, which housed the Irish law courts, and seized several other buildings in Dublin.

For 700 years Irish rebels had fought English rulers. Now Irish rebels were to fight Irish rulers. In June 1922 government troops bombarded the Four Courts, and fighting spread throughout the Free State. Two years of Anglo-Irish war were followed by two years of Irish civil war. Those parts of O'Connell Street that had survived in 1916 were destroyed. Between 1919 and 1921, the British government had hanged or shot 24 Irishmen for taking up arms in the struggle for an independent Ireland; in 1922 and 1923, the new Irish government executed more than three times that number for the same reason.

De Valera remained in the background during the civil war. After it, he re-entered politics, formed a new party, the Fianna Fail, and in 1927 did an about turn. With a wriggling disclaimer of its validity, he took the oath of allegiance to the British Crown, over which so many of his comrades had lost their lives. He renounced force as a means of obtaining independence for the whole of Ireland, and by 1932 he was Prime Minister. His party remained in power for all but eight of the following 35 years. In 1936, taking advantage of England's abdication crisis, the Dail passed an Act whereby the British Crown disappeared for all practical purposes from the Irish constitution. (Its only remaining function was to serve as a formal instrument for accrediting Irish ambassadors to foreign countries.) In 1937, a new Irish constitution set up a "sovereign, independent, democratic state"—a republic in all but name. At last, in 1948, the 26 counties of Ireland were formally declared a republic by an Act of the Irish parliament.

To many Dubliners, the independent republic that had been so bitterly and fervently fought over in the first quarter of the century has proved curiously unsatisfactory. During the Second World War, the government's policy of neutrality meant that Dubliners officially played no part in the struggle against Hitler, unless the despatch of some Dublin fire-engines to Belfast after the Germans blitzed the city in 1941 be accounted a war effort. True, Dubliners were among the 100,000 Irishmen who ignored the official attitude and enlisted individually in the British Army. But after the war, many Dubliners felt uneasy, conscious not only that they had escaped the privations of war-time but that they were missing the spirit of energetic reconstruction that followed. Until well into the Sixties, Dublin was a depressed and isolated capital.

Many of the dreams of 1916 are unfulfilled. The six counties of Northern Ireland remain part of the United Kingdom, still—in the eyes of militant republicans—waiting to be liberated. Bloody rebellion and squalid civil war have not removed the main preoccupation of Irish politics and history—the influence of England—and violence continues, sporadically but persistently. Much has changed, but all too much has remained the same.

The Irish government finds that its birth in violent rebellion has left difficulties. It cannot dishonour the methods by which it came to power, yet it must suppress those methods when they are revived and applied to the same objectives it fought for: a free and united Ireland. De Valera found it necessary to outlaw and jail those of his old comrades who stayed out on the hills, and for years banned mention of the IRA on radio or in the newspapers. An election poster of the refurbished Sinn Fein party in the 1970s pointed up the invidiousness of the government's position. It showed the cabinet then in office: a score of suited gentlemen seated round a polished wooden table. Underneath was the damning caption: "More English than the English themselves."

Nor have the mystic dreams of Pearse come to pass. The liberated, prosperous Gael seems much like other liberated, prosperous Westerners, fond of cars, television, central heating and other tangible benefits. He never took very kindly to the enforced revival of Gaelic, which became a compulsory subject in schools in the 1920s. Nowadays, in spite of the Gaelic names on Dublin's buses and street signs, the Dubliner tends to forget Gaelic as soon as he leaves school and stops having to learn it. His language is English, as is much of his culture. In many ways, Dublin has never been so English. There are more English tourists than ever before, more English money in business and commerce, more English newspapers, magazines and books. Above all—as the fleets of tall aerials crowning the city's houses bear witness—England is showing nightly in the living-rooms of hundreds of thousands of Dubliners. No propaganda of the past was ever as persuasive.

Dublin still lives between two national histories, and her past is the story of an overlap. The result is unique: not Irish in the sense that the cities of Cork or Galway are Irish; certainly not English. Dublin does not fit into a stylized role, nor into any doctrinaire interpretation of Irish history.

Not long ago I watched a scene that brought home this truth. Some young girls were playing in the Garden of Remembrance in Parnell Square. The garden is an architectural curiosity, comprising a cross-shaped pool sunk deep among lawns and flower-beds. Bronze plaques on the railings round the garden proclaim that it was established in memory of those who gave their lives in 1916. The girls were running and twittering on the paths beside the pool, wherever the stolid uniformed keeper could not see them. Whenever he did come into view, they stopped playing and tried to look demure. To them, those revered martyrs of 1916 and of all the centuries of Irish rebellion were as distant as Moses. The freedom so dearly won and so laboriously commemorated here represented to them a grey, heavy, old people's concern, an unnatural symbol of restraint and authority, imposing boredom and dull duties. As I watched their lithe and lively forms running and jumping and breaking all the rules, it seemed to me that Patrick Pearse had had his day.

The Glorious Failure of Easter, 1916

Dubliners examine the charred ruins of the city's General Post Office, which served as the headquarters of the insurgents during the week of the Easter Rising.

Before the 20th Century, Dublin was rarely at the centre of violent insurrections against British rule. This immunity ended suddenly on Easter Monday, April 24, 1916, when about 1,500 ill-armed rebels—members of the para-military Irish Volunteers and the small Irish Citizen Army—seized 14 buildings in the city centre in a bid to establish a free Irish republic. The leaders of the insurrection, which has become known as the Easter Rising, lacked popular support and remained isolated in their strongholds. British troops, using artillery, quickly bombarded them into surrender. But aspirations of independence were not so easy to extinguish, and later, when harsh penalties had been meted out to the rebels, many Dubliners came to see the Rising as one of its leaders, Patrick Pearse, had envisaged it: "The most glorious chapter in the later history of Ireland."

Preparing for Revolution

Nearly two years before the Rising, the Irish Volunteers defied an arms embargo in order to equip themselves for the anticipated clash with Britain. In broad daylight on July 26, 1914, armaments purchased in Hamburg were delivered at Howth, nine miles north of Dublin, on a yacht owned by the author and rebel sympathizer, Erskine Childers. Within an hour, 800 Volunteers were marching back to Dublin with the guns on their shoulders.

Members of the Irish Nationalist Boy Scouts, standing on Howth quay, reach out to help Volunteers unload the consignment of weapons smuggled in from Germany. Many of the scouts served as couriers for the rebels in the Rising.

Mrs. Mary Childers (left) and a friend sit with rifles on board the gun-running yacht. Erskine Childers was later executed after opposing the new Irish government during the civil war that followed Independence in 1921.

A platoon of Irish Volunteers in civilian dress stand to attention with some of the 900 second-hand Mauser rifles they have just received at Howth harbour.

Kitted out in dark green uniforms with white bandoleers, men of the Irish Citizen Army parade with illegal arms at the edge of Croydon Park, Dublin, in 1915.

A section of the Metropole Hotel in Sackville Street—now O'Connell Street—collapses after the explosion of a shell intended for the General Post Office nearby. The army's methodical shelling totally destroyed more than 170 buildings in the city centre.

British troops (below) fire at a rebel target from a barricade that was originally erected by the insurgents themselves. By the time the fighting had ended, 450 people had been killed. More than a hundred of the fatalities were British.

Manning the Barricades

Wasting no time in dealing with the insurgents, the British rushed massive reinforcements to their Dublin garrison; by mid-week, their forces in the city stood at 12,000 men. With Trinity College as their base, the troops surrounded the inner city, severing contact between rebel strongholds and bombarding buildings with incendiary shells whose flames spread rapidly. By Sunday, fire, artillery and hunger forced the rebels into an unconditional surrender.

A phalanx of rebels, captured after the failure of the Easter Rising, is marched under escort along Eden Quay before deportation to prisons in England.

Days of Reckoning

In the month that followed the Rising, the British arrested thousands of rebels and their sympathizers, many of whom were sent to prisons in England and Wales. After a series of courts martial, 15 insurgent leaders were put before the firing squad. Although they had at first been reviled by the public for the chaos and bloodshed they caused, the executed men were viewed as martyrs, and those who returned from imprisonment were hailed as heroes.

In a photograph thought to have been taken secretly by a warder, the rebel leader Joseph Plunkett stands blindfolded before the firing squad at Kilmainham Jail.

On one of their thrice-weekly visits, relatives bring news and presents to the rebels temporarily interned at Richmond Barracks on the outskirts of Dublin.

A Gaelic banner proclaims a welcome for Countess Markievicz, a charismatic Irish insurgent married to a Polish count, after her release from prison in 1917.

Sacred Heart
of Jesus
I place my trust
in Thee

4

The Legacy of St. Patrick

To many Dubliners, the name of Matt Talbot is sacred. Pilgrims come each day to pray before his sumptuous marble shrine in the Church of Our Lady of Lourdes, in Sean MacDermott Street; and for some time now the Roman Catholic Church has been considering the case for his canonization. Yet Matt Talbot was no more than a humble dock labourer, and to begin with he was bad. Like many others living in the decayed slums of north Dublin during the second half of the last century, he had little chance of being anything else. He was 12 when he first got violently drunk—which was by no means precocious for those days—and in the 16 years that followed, he drank and gambled away the meagre wages he earned working on the docks.

His Road to Damascus was the backyard of a pub where, having been refused a loan by his despairing mates, he saw a dog sniffing at an empty bottle. The dog looked up with an expression of cringing appeal, and Matt recognized in that abject creature the figure he cut among his acquaintances. Overnight, he reformed. He worked hard, and was kind and considerate to his friends. All who lived in the district knew they could call on Matt if they were in trouble. But he did not forget how bad he had been. He gave up drink, of course, and he renounced all other indulgences. He slept for no more than four hours a night, thus allowing additional time for prayer, and what little repose he did permit himself was taken on a wooden plank, with a timber block for a pillow.

His meals consisted of bread, occasionally buttered or dipped in the water in which a fish had been boiled, and a mixture of cold tea and cocoa drunk without milk or sugar. He evinced no interest in sex; and the closest he came to marriage was when the cook in his lodging-house proposed to him. After nine days of prayer he told the lady that God had dictated a negative answer. When he died in 1925, at the age of 69, it was found that for years he had crimped his body with iron chains.

Matt was almost unknown during his lifetime, but within a few years of his death his modest grave in Glasnevin cemetery became a national shrine. Canonization was proposed in 1931, and in 1952 his remains were transferred to a special vault at Glasnevin. Twenty years later, they were brought to their present resting place in the Church of Our Lady of Lourdes. Theologians are still sieving and weighing the abundant testimony to Matt's posthumous wonder-working, for a saint is only declared when it can be proved to the Vatican's satisfaction that he has interceded with God in Heaven to bring blessings to those still on earth. Dubliners

Flanked by everlasting blooms, a statue of Jesus extends welcoming arms within a glass weather-shield in busy O'Connell Street. There are many such shrines in Dublin—perhaps the most devoutly Catholic city in the world.

themselves, however, have no doubt about Matt's sanctity; there are regular masses, novenas, appeals and petitions aimed at securing for him what are called "the honours of the altar".

Matt is venerated because he epitomizes the virtues that Irish Catholics love to love, if not to emulate. He was regenerate, poor, industrious, ascetic, self-effacing and chaste to the point of asexuality. He chastized his body. He often expressed regret for the trouble he had caused his mother during the days of his dissipation. He was of the people and always behaved as a good, if somewhat retiring, neighbour. Above all, he believed unquestioningly in the ultimate goodness of God's mysterious ways. Apart from Matt's virtues, however, it is difficult to find anything else of interest to say about him. He was the very opposite of a stage Irishman, and to a non-believer his devoutly penitential but singularly lacklustre existence makes him seem the quintessence of insignificance. In other Catholic countries, such as Spain and Italy, the heroes of the Church tend to be rather spunkier figures.

Irish Catholicism is on its own in other ways, for Christianity's development in Ireland has differed from that in other European countries. The new religion was brought to much of Europe, including Britain, by the occupying Roman administration. But Ireland was never conquered by the Romans and Christianity arrived there, early in the 5th Century, unsupported by troops and untainted by colonialism.

Credit for bringing the new faith to the island is usually given to St. Patrick, who as a boy was kidnapped from his home in Scotland by Irish marauders. After escaping, he returned to Ireland in the year 432 to convert his captors. Patrick remains a shadowy figure, however, and it is likely that much of the evangelizing spadework was done by others, especially monks fleeing from the barbarian invasions of Gaul and Wales.

In any event, Christianity went straight to the hearts of the Irish. The monastery was very similar to the basic unit of Celtic society—a kind of super-family—and within its precincts the sexes were allowed to mix in a way that would have been unthinkable later. Monastic Christianity also blended easily with other qualities of the Celtic realm: the Irish loved learning and story-telling, and monks brought them the art of writing, the steely precision of the Latin tongue and a corpus of scriptural dramas, dogmas and disputes.

Christian tales were merged with pagan, so that godly evangelists were credited with exploits—murders, warfare, contests of arms and the like— more readily associated with lusty heathens. There was also a tendency to invest traditional Irish heroes and heroines with the saintly virtues of the Gospel figures. The partly legendary St. Brigid, for example, whose origins certainly go back to pagan times, was credited with some of the qualities of the Virgin Mary.

The Church, in turn, borrowed rustic touches from the Celtic imagina-

A man pushing a battered pram raises his hat in respect as he passes the steps of St. Mary's Pro-Cathedral, the principal Roman Catholic church of Dublin. St. Mary's only has the status of a provisional or Pro-Cathedral because Catholics hope that Christ Church Cathedral, which has been in Protestant hands since the time of the Reformation, will once again become the main centre of Catholic worship in the city.

tion to add to its own lore: a bird that dropped a feather for a hermit in need of a pen; a stag that allowed a travelling preacher to use its antlers as a lectern—and a fly that marked the place in the Bible while the preacher enlarged on the point he had just read out. St. Patrick himself is said to have explained the nature of the Trinity with the help of a shamrock leaf.

Two attitudes of profound and lasting significance also seem to have taken root in the Irish Church during this early period. One was a chosen-race complex, compensation perhaps for a nation on the remotest periphery of the known world; the picture that chroniclers presented of Irish godliness makes it seem almost as if Ireland, rather than Palestine, was the setting of the New Testament story. (One poem goes so far as to speak of how St. Brigid dandled the young Christ on her knee.) The second attitude that came to permeate the Irish mentality was an almost schizoid ambivalence towards women—the sex that, infuriatingly to the religious zealot, combines the virtues of the Blessed Virgin with the vices of the seductress Eve. Thus a devout regard for Holy Mary, Brigid and other saintly women was counterbalanced by a sometimes confused, usually hostile and often priggish view of women in general. This latter view predated Irish Christianity. "Women should be dreaded like fire and feared like wild beasts," declared the 4th-Century Irish king, Cormac the Wise, "for they are moths for tenacity, serpents for cunning, bad among the good and worse among the bad."

Christians took up Cormac's theme with vigour. St. Brendan, a 6th-Century figure, is said to have cursed and whipped with carriage reins a girl who approached him "wanting to play her game with him". His contemporary, St. Kevin of Glendalough, went even further. When a lady followed him to his hermitage, he hurled her over a cliff. The Irish love motherhood, but have always been reserved about the steps that necessarily precede it; and women as enigmatic vessels both of sin and virtue recur frequently in the annals of Irish Catholicism.

In its isolation from the rest of Christian Europe, the Irish Church often demonstrated an independence that angered the papacy. There was a major clash, for example, over Ireland's insistence on sticking to its own traditional dating of Easter. Far more disturbing to Rome was the Irish tendency to produce suspect theologians. One of the most famous heretics of the 4th and 5th Centuries, generally regarded as an Irishman, was Pelagius, whose denial of the doctrine of original sin led to his excommunication in 418.

The Irish sense of being separate and special was reinforced during the 7th and 8th Centuries, when western Europe was ravaged by barbarian invasions from the east. Ireland again remained inviolate, and the Irish Church was able to achieve a degree of learning and piety that outshone Rome itself—ensuring that at least an ember of civilization was kept glowing throughout the 200 years of Europe's Dark Ages.

Ireland's splendid isolation drew to an end with the arrival of Viking longboats in the late 8th and 9th Centuries. Although the Norsemen almost succeeded in subduing the whole island, they had little effect on the Irish Church, and after Brian Boru's great victory at the Battle of Clontarf in 1014, most of the Norse settlers converted to Christianity. Then, in 1169, came the Norman English. On the face of it, the English conquest of Ireland brought together two peoples who shared the same religion: a Catholicism that acknowledged, if it did not always act on, the supremacy of the Pope. Behind this apparent unity, however, differences of language, culture and tradition stamped the religious attitudes of each race.

The division was formalized in the 16th Century, when Henry VIII tried by armed force to extend the English Reformation to Ireland. Like the language and lore of the Gaels, Irish Catholicism seemed doomed to extinction as Henry dissolved the Irish monasteries, took over their lands and treasure, and tried to impose his own brand of Protestantism in place of "the usurped authority of the Bishop of Rome". But Irish Catholicism showed more resilience than the Irish language. The religion became a symbol and rallying-point for the great mass of the Irish people, marking them off both from the English and from that adoptive colonial élite, the Anglo-Irish. To the present day, Catholicism has remained a hallmark of the Gael, an anchoring identity in the bitter relationship that has existed between the two countries.

In its struggle to withstand that relationship, however, Irish Catholicism became increasingly rigid and authoritarian. The priests alone were

Depicted by a Victorian artist in stained glass, the patriarchal figure of St. Patrick, the patron saint of Ireland, presides over the choir of St. Patrick's Cathedral. Legend has it that Patrick was snatched from his home in Scotland by Irish raiders and brought to Ireland as a slave. Escaping to Gaul, he dreamed that the Irish begged him "to come and walk among us once more", and around the year 432 he returned as a missionary. He is said to have baptized some followers close to where the cathedral now stands.

qualified to educate—which they frequently did at the risk of their lives—and they most of all suffered at the hands of the invaders. As a result, the Irish people offered them willing and absolute obedience. The priests, in turn, provided a philosophy for surviving the hardships and humiliations imposed by the godless English.

Some inkling of those hardships is provided by an 18th-Century English traveller. "A landlord in Ireland," he wrote, "can scarcely invent an order which a servant or labourer dares to refuse to execute. Nothing satisfies him but an unlimited submission. Disrespect, or anything tending towards sauciness, he may punish with his cane or his horsewhip with the most perfect security; a poor man would have his bones broke if he offered to lift his hands in his own defence. Knocking-down is spoken of in the country in a manner that makes an Englishman stare."

One can see Ireland as the hapless child of a marriage between two dominant influences—England and Rome. The marriage terminated with the Reformation, and Ireland, it has been said, was between the Devil and the Holy See. Geography gave the Devil physical custody, but Ireland's heart remained faithful to its Holy Father in Rome. The Irish have always seen Popes in a rosier light than the Italians who live with them do, and at times their efforts to please the leader of the Church have gone far beyond his own expectations. Unfortunately for the Irish, however, the Holy Father has not always returned their loyalty.

The Anglo-Normans who conquered Ireland in the 12th Century did so with the enthusiastic support of the papacy, which hoped to curb the independence of the Irish Church. And on several occasions since then, the Pope, for political reasons, has found it expedient to plump for English interests rather than Irish aspirations. Irish parish priests often risked their lives and livings to side with those who rebelled against English rule; and certainly no rebel would ever have doubted that Christ, the Holy Ghost, the Blessed Virgin (in particular) and all the saints were on his side. But the Irish bishops were more likely to take their cue from Rome, and this usually meant backing the established power of England, condemning any resort to arms, and even excommunicating patriot heroes. Eamon de Valera, who dominated Irish public life for more than 30 years, was one so treated, though he was reinstated when his political position seemed beyond challenge.

Throughout the 19th Century, the Vatican's main interest in Ireland was as a pathway towards the redemption of apostate England. But Irish independence would have blocked that path, and all attempts to achieve it were accordingly discouraged. Ironically, the campaign of redemption was launched, not by Irish Catholics in England, but by English Protestants in Ireland. Throughout the 1850s and 1860s, hordes of English Hot Gospellers descended on Dublin to rescue young slum-dwellers, such as Matt Talbot, from the shackles of "papist superstition". Offering free soup

Cathedral in Conflict

Established in the 12th Century, St. Patrick's Cathedral has had an uneasy relationship with English authority. In 1540, the cathedral clergy were locked up for resisting the Protestant Reformation of Henry VIII. The King not only turned St. Patrick's into a temple of the new faith, but also seized the cathedral's revenues. St. Patrick's suffered another blow in 1643 when Oliver Cromwell's Puritan troopers occupied it—and stabled their horses in the aisles.

But it is with the name of Jonathan Swift, the Irish patriot and satirist, that the cathedral is mainly associated. Swift was Dean from 1713 until 1745. For two days after his death, Dubliners filed past his coffin, and he was buried—"as privately as possible and at twelve o'clock at night", according to his wishes—in the cathedral's nave.

Boys of St. Patrick's choir school help to maintain the cathedral's tradition of fine choral singing.

The massive bulk of St. Patrick's Cathedral looms against the grey winter sky. Extensively restored in 1864, the building is 300 feet long and 67 feet wide.

and schooling, as well as sanctimony and salvation, these missionaries drew scathing rebukes from the Catholic Church. "Education, charity, the Bible, are now inscribed upon the banners of those whose bigotry and fanaticism in past days delighted in persecution and in blood," wrote Paul Cullen, Archbishop of Dublin, in a pastoral letter of 1856. "Under these false colours, assumed for the purpose of deception, a system of pecuniary proselytism, having for its object to make converts by bribes and gold, has been established by the many bigoted and fanatical haters of Catholicity who abound . . . and an active and insidious war is carried on against our ancient and venerable Church."

Dublin was a place of constant hunger in those days, and it was inevitable that some members of Archbishop Cullen's flock should have succumbed to the blandishments of the "Soupers". But most Dubliners clung to their faith with a tenacity that time seems to have left undiminished. Sean O'Casey, who was born in 1880 and—though Protestant himself—grew up in Matt Talbot's mainly Catholic neighbourhood, thought of his native city as being "more sacred than Rome; as holy as Zion". If the young O'Casey were to walk through Dublin today, he would be unlikely to change his opinion. It is impossible to travel far in any direction without coming upon a Catholic church, where the schedule of masses often reads something like a railway timetable.

In the centre of the city, houses, terraces, whole streets even, are given over to church organizations: schools, mission headquarters, seminaries, orders of monks or nuns. There are Catholic bookshops where the

A Dublin priest is served lunch by his housekeeper. Such ladies, noted for their impeccable respectability and tight-lipped discretion, play a leading role in the life of the Catholic community. Their tasks range from visiting the sick and the elderly to organizing knitting and sewing clubs for the benefit of foreign missions.

merchandise ranges from tomes of abstruse theology and volumes recording the work of the Irish mission in Macau to pamphlets bearing such titles as *Fatima in Focus, What is Faith?* and *The Legacy of St. Vincent de Paul.* There are shops specializing in priestly vestments, where the latest clerical collars and lightweight cassocks from the United States can be bought by priests with an eye to fashion. Travel agents fill their windows with offers of cheap package tours to Lourdes—the only trip abroad that many Dubliners will make.

On foot and in buses, people cross themselves as they pass churches, shrines, or—puzzling to the non-Irish observer—one of the unmarked sites where some hero of the political turmoil of the early 1920s was killed. Conversation is laced with phrases of religious import, often tacked on to a word automatically, meaninglessly, adding nothing but a spurious aura of piety. Speak of a dead man and "God rest his soul" or some such petition will be tossed in after each mention of his name. Things happen "with the help of God" or "God willing" or "by Heaven and all the holy saints".

Similar pieties recur in the newspapers, which carry special Thanksgiving columns for the acknowledgement of blessings received. "Grateful thanks," reads a typical entry, "to St. Jude for health restored and job obtained." St. Jude, apostle and martyr, appears regularly, but other entries reflect the shifting trends of Dublin iconography. "Grateful thanks to Matt Talbot, St. Francis Xavier and Pope John for wonderful favours." (Pope John was a favourite from the first. In a room I once rented in Dublin, his photograph and one of President Kennedy flanked a penetrating portrait of Jesus.)

Statues and images, sometimes provided with permanently lighted electrical haloes, have helped to establish many saints as personal acquaintances who can be appealed to and bargained with on terms of easy familiarity. "Holy St. Christopher," runs a popular invocation, "help me now in my present and urgent position and, in return, I promise to make your name known and cause you to be invoked. Publication promised." The publication refers to the formal thanks that will appear in the same column should the prayer prove successful. This kind of appeal points not only to the Irishman's love of a deal, but also suggests an unexpected desire for publicity on the part of the saints.

The In Memoriam columns are a natural repository for outpourings of emotion, much of it expressed in clumsily mawkish but wholly unmockable doggerel along the lines of "I see you sit beside me there: next time I look the seat is bare." Similar sentiments find more lasting expression on the tombstones of the city's cemeteries, of which the largest and grandest is Matt Talbot's former resting place, two miles north of O'Connell Bridge. Although the graveyard is generally called Glasnevin, after the surrounding suburb, its official title of Prospect Cemetery, from the name of a former estate, seems more eloquent of the Irish belief in life after death.

Most illustrious Irishmen over the past hundred years have been laid to rest here, including the patriots Charles Stewart Parnell, Michael Collins, Arthur Griffith and Daniel O'Connell, who is commemorated by a massive 160-foot high round tower that stands just inside the cemetery gates. Beyond the tower stretches what seems to be a vast petrified forest: 50 acres of pillars, obelisks, domes and cupolas in the lugubrious grey of Wicklow granite. Although a huge tonnage of stone is already lurching or crumbling well before the Day of Judgement, some of the newer graves reflect the whims of funerary fashion. Oval-framed photographs of the deceased are set into tombstones and glass-domed displays of synthetic horticulture spread waxen glory over beds of green marble chippings. The Irishman's home is his coffin, says Leopold Bloom, the wandering Dublin Jew of James Joyce's *Ulysses*, and the sombre elaborations of Glasnevin tend to affirm the opinion.

One immediate consequence of Irish Independence in 1921 was the exodus of thousands of Protestants to England. Some anticipated a reversion to barbarism, others a pogrom. In the event, their fears proved to be unfounded. The Catholics, having played the role of the oppressed for so long, showed no desire to become the oppressors. Indeed, when Ireland severed its remaining links with the British Crown in 1937, it elected a Protestant, Douglas Hyde, as its first president. Another Protestant, Erskine Childers, served as head of state in 1973-74. In spite of occasional complaints of discrimination by both Protestants and Catholics, the Irish approach to religion is generally acknowledged on both sides to be exemplary.

As well as guaranteeing freedom of conscience and worship, the constitutions of 1922 and 1937 were also careful to emphasize the non-denominational character of the Irish State. It is true that a clause contained in the 1937 constitution acknowledged "the special position" of the Catholic Church as "the guardian of the Faith professed by the great majority of the citizens". But the clause amounted to little more than pious ornamentation, and when it was dropped in 1973, there was not a murmur of clerical dissent.

Lack of a privileged legal status, however, has not prevented the Catholic Church from bringing its influence to bear over a wide range of social issues. It insists, for example, upon the education of Catholic children in Catholic schools, which means that, although the government provides money and lays down academic criteria, most schools are under denominational ownership and control. There are many, including teachers, who regard the system as antiquated, undemocratic and divisive. Yet, whenever the question of non-denominational education is raised—as it frequently is—the Dublin press is deluged with letters of protest. "I should be horrified," wrote one anguished mother recently, "at the thought of my children attending a school where classes would not begin with a Hail Mary. How could a Catholic teacher feel he was dealing adequately with the history of the 20th Century without mentioning the message of Fatima, for Catholics immeasurably the most significant occurrence of recent history?"

One of the hardest fought battles between opponents and supporters of clerical control has been over the issue of censorship. Ireland was not the first country to introduce censorship laws, but the Irish Censorship of Publications Board, from the moment of its appointment in 1929 until well into the 1970s, displayed a pietistic fervour and philistinism that probably did as much damage to the country's reputation as the activities of the IRA. In little more than 40 years, these officious and autocratic Grundies managed to ban more than 10,000 books, ranging from the autobiography of Tallulah Bankhead to the collected papers of Sigmund Freud. The objection in both cases, and in most others, was that the books contained sexually explicit passages.

There was hardly any author of note whose name did not figure in the Board's blacklist, and many of Ireland's own great writers—James Joyce, Sean O'Casey, Frank O'Connor, Samuel Beckett, Sean O'Faolain—who won fame abroad, were stigmatized with the labels of "indecent" or "obscene" at home. As the Irish playwright Paul Vincent Carroll once observed, "Government censorship is pernicious and even foolish, for it has admitted to the nation that historical stranger, the Puritan, and in fact presented him with the freedom of Dublin city."

In recent years, though, the Puritan has been forced to loosen his grip, and the Irish are now absorbing—without evident signs of corruption—many of the books that have long been regarded as classics elsewhere. Thankfully, the new tolerance does not yet extend to outright pornography and, after running the drearily salacious gauntlet of so many London newsagents, I find it refreshing to enter a Dublin newspaper shop. Here the only full-frontal exposure is of magazines devoted to, say, politics, or bicycling, or female fashion, and the most scabrous literature is of a kind considered *risqué* in England more than 20 years ago: gauche stories of adulteries, rapes and orgies, illustrated by no more than line drawings, with shadows or obstructions fulfilling the erstwhile function of the fig-leaf.

More controversial are the laws relating to divorce, abortion and contraception. The first two are illegal, as is the sale, though not the use, of contraceptives. In fact, there are ways around each of these barriers. Those with money and know-how can always leave to take up temporary residence in England or Northern Ireland in order to obtain a divorce.

For couples forbidden by conscience to seek a divorce, there remains the possibility of ecclesiastical annullment. In order to be granted a decree of nullity, however, it is necessary to prove not only that one of the partners is totally incapable of understanding or fulfilling the basic demands of the married state, but also that the incapacity existed at the time the marriage occurred. These are, of course, hard conditions to satisfy, so it is hardly surprising that of the 800 or so nullity applications heard each year, fewer than 15 per cent are granted.

Both the abortion and contraception barriers can also be sidestepped with a ticket to England or to the North. And because of a curious legal anomaly that allows contraceptives to be imported by the sackful, a flourishing under-the-counter trade has grown up in Dublin and other large cities. Since the early 1960s, the birth-control pill has come into increasingly widespread use among Irish women. The pill was condemned by the Vatican in 1968, but many doctors have gone on prescribing it as the remedy for a host of imaginary ailments.

The fact that avenues of escape exist is no consolation to those who oppose the law. Is it tolerable, asked one of the speakers during a recent parliamentary debate on birth-control legislation, "that the laws of the state should taint with criminality . . . matters which a minority of citizens—not necessarily a religious minority—regard as morally justified and their own personal concern?"

These laws fall most heavily on women; and they are seen by feminist groups as yet another manifestation of that notorious and perplexing phenomenon: the Irish male psyche. It may not be true—as the old joke has it—that an Irishman would clamber over a dozen naked women to reach his bottle of Guinness, but his attitude towards sex and marriage was, until recently, idiosyncratic. As late as the 1950s Ireland had the lowest marriage rate in the Western world. In addition, it was not at all unusual for couples to wed long past middle age. "We suggest," wrote the Catholic journal *Ave Maria*, in evident seriousness, "that all culpable Irish bachelors in country districts be taken into custody and held in prison until such time as they make a promise to find a mate within six months. This may seem drastic, but Ireland's falling population, due to infrequent marriages, calls for definite action to diminish bachelorhood."

Fortunately, such action has proved to be unnecessary. Increasing affluence and urbanization have helped to break down the old sexual apartheid, and Irish marriage patterns are now drawing closer to those of other West European countries. Nevertheless, the Irishman from whom modern affluence remains remote still shows a greater reluctance to marry than his European counterpart; and having taken the plunge, he often seems to display more interest in drinking, horse-racing and football than in the pleasures of the connubial bed. The large size of Irish families is proof enough that sex occurs, but one suspects that the wits are not too wide of the mark in explaining this away as "procreation without recreation".

If Irishmen tend to neglect their wives, however, it is different with their mothers. A mother personifies the female virtues, but has none of the female vices. She is a woman to love and not to fear; a selfless provider, not a demanding taker; an adoring Madonna, not a seductive Eve. A

A visitor to Our Lady of Lourdes grotto in Dublin (above) pauses before an array of red electric candles. Instead of lighting a candle in the traditional way, worshippers can place a coin in a meter and—like the woman on the right, near the entrance to the grotto—press a button to light up the bulbs. The grotto contains a piece of stone brought from Lourdes in France and said to possess healing properties.

wife will reach her own apotheosis when she, too, becomes a mother. And if she has a son, the chances are that she will try to steer him well away from the slippery slopes of courtship and romance, seeing him rather as the Madonna saw her own son—as a lover, not of women, but of the world. (Most of all, until recently she wanted him to be a priest.) Thus it continues: mothers and sons, husbands and wives, bound by an enduring, if sometimes betrayed, allegiance to the Church's ideal of chastity.

In this predominantly Catholic city one can come surprisingly often on some silent, neglected church. Its doors will be permanently locked, its windows will be wired up, and its pews will be gathering dust. Such forlorn relics belong not, of course, to the Church of Rome, but to that misnamed and ailing support of the Protestant Ascendancy, the Church of Ireland.

The Chapel Royal in Dublin Castle provides more poignant testimony to the Church of Ireland's declining strength and status. The Chapel was adapted for Catholic worship in 1943, and the atmosphere and artefacts of Rome blend oddly with the patrician Anglo-Irish splendours of the 18th Century. Around the balcony of this sombre masterpiece hang the names and emblems of former Lords Lieutenant of Ireland, a roll-call of the English aristocracy: Sidney, Essex, Strafford, Grafton, Northumberland.

Yet on the walls there is a modern version of the 12 Stations of the Cross, and at the back of the church a notice-board announces masses and novenas, and gives details of the traditional Catholic pilgrimage to Lough Derg, the remote lake in the west of Ireland where St. Patrick is said to have had a vision of purgatory. No less incongruous to Protestant eyes are five flags displayed above the organ. They belonged to Irish regiments that helped the French achieve their victory over Britain at the Battle of Fontenoy in 1745.

No clash of loyalties defaces the walls of St. Patrick's Cathedral, where Jonathan Swift, the mordant author of *Gulliver's Travels*, was dean. Though the Cathedral has recently made itself available for the services of other denominations, its tone and atmosphere remain staunchly, if somewhat hollowly, Protestant. Here the incongruities are between the interior—a hymn to imperial England—and the surrounding tenements. Plaques and cartouches comprise a marble archive of the achievement, pride and ideals of the Empire. For example, over the grave of Thomas Rice Henn—who perished in 1880, aged 31, "on the fatal field of Maiwand in Afghanistan"—are inscribed the words of his commander, Sir Garnet Wolseley: "No hero ever died more nobly than he did. I envy the manner of his death. If I had ten sons I should indeed be proud if all ten fell as he fell."

Similar Augustan sentiments commemorate the dead heroes of—to reproduce their archaic, orotund spelling—Lasware, Hindostan, Inkerman, Balaclava, the China War of the 1840s, the Birmah War of the 1850s, Egypt, Palestine, Flanders. That the Chinese War was fought to revive the

The window of a Dublin travel agency reflects the specialized tastes of Catholic customers. Advertisements for trips to Irish beauty spots are overshadowed by signs giving information about excursions to places of particular religious significance: Lourdes, Fatima in Portugal and, of course, Rome, the Eternal City.

opium trade and trounce the Chinese because they were perverse enough to want it banned, or that, at much the same time, many Irishmen were being forced by famine to emigrate or die, are unrecorded details. Here in the cathedral all is sweetness and self-congratulation. Carved in softly flattering alabaster, marquises and bishops, judges and generals, face one another in all the panoply of state.

A more accurate tableau would show that the urbane piety of the Ascendancy was often entwined with rancour and bigotry. Though they held all the power and money, the Anglo-Irish Protestants were always a small minority; and they were well aware that, at any moment, the Catholic hordes might rise up against them. It is said that William Magee, Protestant Archbishop of Dublin during the 1820s, was so fearful of this eventuality that he refused to consecrate any church that was not capable of serving as a fortress.

Protestants feared and abominated the orientally lurid colours of Catholic vestments, the use of the talisman rosary, the spraying of diabolical Byzantine aromas, the ringing of the Sanctus bell, the "idolatrous" veneration of statues and sacred relics, and the incomprehensible chanting of Italianate Latin. Such rites and practices savoured of superstition, and seemed to endanger the rational, open conduct of Protestant relations with the Almighty.

A Protestant rector, and grandfather of the playwright J. M. Synge, boasted in old age that he had dedicated his life "to waging war against popery in its thousand forms of wickedness". His fanaticism was commonplace (as it still is among many of the Protestants of Belfast). When Thomas Carlyle, that lapidary sage of English Toryism, visited Ireland in 1840, he recorded the thoughts that came to him during a Church of Ireland service one Sunday: "I felt how decent English Protestants, or the sons of such, might with zealous affection like to assemble here once a week, and remind themselves of English purities and decencies and Gospel ordinances, in the midst of a black howling Babel of superstitious savagery—like Hebrews sitting by the streams of Babel. . . ."

For Protestants of the Ascendancy, it was no great hardship to be surrounded by this crimson sea of popery. They luxuriated in privilege and self-righteousness. They interbred, avoiding the contaminating dilution of papist blood; and if the choice among their own number became too limited, England made good the deficit. The British Army in Ireland was a fertile source of suitable sires; and England itself provided a happy hunting ground for Anglo-Irish males in search of wives.

But then, in 1921, the crimson sea crashed over the red-white-and-blue storm barrier, and Catholic Ireland came into its own. This cataclysm not only ended Protestant supremacy, it also struck a death blow at Irish Protestantism itself. Reduced by the departure of thousands of their co-religionists, and no longer able to look to England for fresh infusions of blood, those Protestants who remained behind had only two alternatives: to cross the great divide and marry Catholics, or to succumb to a statistically increasing sterility. Either way, their numbers would diminish still further.

The overriding concern of the Protestant community, however, was its relationship with the new Catholic ascendancy. For the first 20 years this proceeded with immaculate, if muted, cordiality. But in 1942 Dr. John Charles McQuaid became Catholic Archbishop of Dublin and Primate of Ireland, and Protestants began to wonder if they had not been right, after all, in equating Home Rule with Rome Rule. During his 31-year Primacy, Dr. McQuaid campaigned unceasingly on behalf of the Dublin poor, securing a vast expansion in schools, housing and welfare facilities.

Not all of his prodigious efforts, however, seemed quite so charitable. He was responsible for the decree that made it "a mortal sin" for Catholics within his diocese to attend Trinity College, Dublin, without special permission. And he it was who played the leading role in quashing the government's plans to provide a free medical service for mothers and for children under the age of 16, arguing that the state would be taking powers "in direct opposition to the rights of the family and the individual".

The tragedy was that, for all his vigour, McQuaid looked backwards, to what he saw as the virtues of the Middle Ages. He was fighting with medieval weapons against the advance of a Brave New World—"the disintegrating culture," as he put it, "that is now ending logically in chaos". Many were behind him, not least the Censorship Board and other bodies concerned with public morals. But as the Protestant-owned *Irish Times* said of McQuaid in 1966, "To those outside his flock he represents the very incarnation of all that it was believed Pope John with his loving heart was trying to rid his Church of—obscurantism, self-righteousness, arrogance and spiritual apartheid."

McQuaid himself, who had returned from Rome only a short time before, told his flock, "You may have been worried by much talk of changes to come. Allow me to reassure you. No change will worry the tranquillity of your Christian lives." But change was already well under way even before McQuaid's retirement. For two decades Ireland had been building up to its own belated industrial revolution, and one result was the rise of a new Catholic middle class that preferred to think and act for itself. Young lawyers, politicians, business executives and media men settled in smart new estates, bought smart new cars, and took up smart new ideas.

The filtered findings of Darwin, Einstein and Freud broke on their world like revelations. No more was a career in the Church the apple of every clever boy's eye. No more was the doctrine of a Catholic élite to be accepted without question. "In the last few years," wrote one of Dublin's most respected journalists in 1966, "an enormous psychological change has occurred in Ireland. The conviction that things could be improved has dawned on a people conditioned to believe that they could only get worse."

The vibrations of revolt, which had already touched every other Western city, also arrived at last in Dublin. Television and ease of travel brought voguish ideologies to poor as well as rich, and the conformity of dissent that affects so many Western countries is evident in Ireland too. Dublin's youngsters do not wear Irish tweeds; they wear jeans. Many find drink and drugs more appealing than holy water. They do not go to church with the regularity of their elders (though before examinations a number of congregations are swollen by the influx of young people). They like speed, freedom and noise. In little more than a decade, the quality of Dublin's noise has changed. At one time it was incidental, natural, Irish—a blend of conversation, laughter, drunks singing, old clanking cars whose exhausts had dropped off from exhaustion. Today's noise is different. It is aggressive, purposeful, international: silencers deliberately removed from motor bikes; shouts uttered, not to communicate, but to shock.

In streets, cafés and dance halls, boys and girls talk noisily, with a kind of unisex *machismo*, making loud and frequent use of four-letter words. In the northern suburbs, among the cold, ugly tenements, or on the bleak and windswept tarmac beside the church where good Matt Talbot sleeps, they get drunk on cider, cuff one another round the ears, steal an old woman's handbag, pirate a car, and climax the evening by overturning it on the wasteland next to Amiens Street station. Some listen with interest to the Marxists, anarchists, nihilists and IRA Provisionals. They speak with Irish accents (which seem ill-fitted to surly, anti-social purposes) but their words are echoes of words in New York, Hamburg, Milan.

"By Jesus and all the Saints!" exclaim their fathers. "Was it for this that Patrick Pearse and James Connolly gave their lives for Ireland?" But paternal protests are drowned in the new cacophony. The old enemies are enemies no more. The Church of Ireland is a tired charger put out to grass. England is indifferent. The victory over both has been eclipsed by new threats, so that some older people have come to accord England a kind of educational function. Typically, the father of a friend of mine rose in fury before his television set when the programme became explicitly sexual. "Turn it off," he shouted. "Whisht," said his wife, matter-of-factly. "That's no Irish programme. It's from the BBC." "Oh, is it so?" said her husband, resuming his seat to see the programme through. To him, the sins of overseas served to stress the virtues of the homeland.

The Church is still powerful enough to draw thousands to the altar each Sunday, and to influence parents, teachers, businessmen, newspaper editors, broadcasters and politicians. But each group has its dissidents, and each year their numbers increase. Ireland can no longer claim to be the island of saints and scholars. Certainly the censers jangle, and hymns and "Hail Marys" ascend daily from the faithful. But outside the churches, a tide is rising that all the priests and nuns and monks of Dublin may be unable to stem.

Servants of God and the Community

PHOTOGRAPHS BY JOHN McDERMOTT

Novices, postulants and professed Sisters—wearing habits denoting their various degrees of admission into the Irish Sisters of Charity—pray at vespers.

One of the most visible signs of Dublin's Catholic heritage is the prevalence of nuns—members of 60 different orders in all, housed in 139 convents and engaged in activities that range from contemplative quietude to tireless charity work. Perhaps the most socially committed of the orders is the Congregation of the Religious Sisters of Charity—better known simply as the Irish Sisters of Charity. Founded in 1815 by Mary Aikenhead, who had been born into a Protestant family but converted to Catholicism at the age of 15, the Sisters were the first religious group in the country to make it their principal aim to help the disadvantaged. They run 18 primary and 10 secondary schools in Dublin, and perform a variety of services for the sick, the aged and alcoholics that, in a more secular society, would be done largely by social workers in the employ of the state.

Standing in front of a skeleton that serves as a teaching aid, a Sister instructs 20 students enrolled in St. Vincent's School of Radiography.

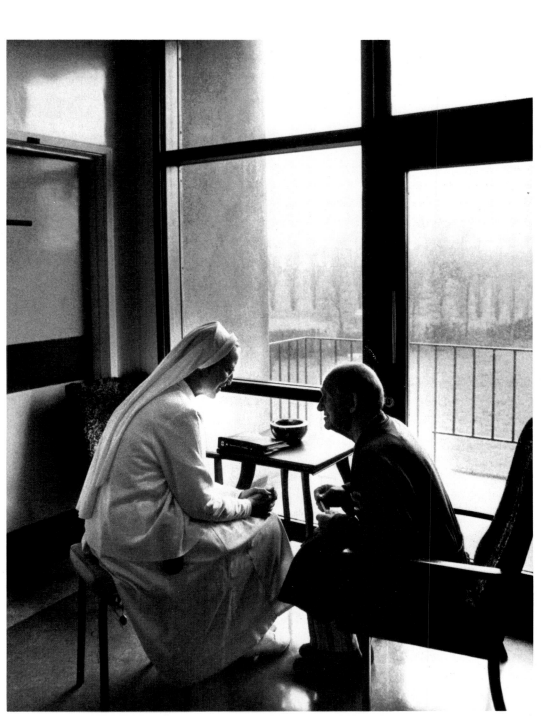

In a sunny room at St. Vincent's, a Sister discusses the future with a patient who will soon leave the hospital.

Healing the Sick

In 1834, Ireland's first Catholic hospital, St. Vincent's, was founded in Dublin by the Irish Sisters of Charity. Today, members of the order help run a total of six hospitals in the city; but St. Vincent's, with 450 beds and an ambitious teaching programme, remains their chief undertaking. More than 11,000 patients are admitted to it every year—and four times as many attend the hospital's various clinics as out-patients.

In one of the surgical wards of St. Vincent's, a Sister changes a dressing for a patient whose bed has been adorned with a get-well card from his granddaughter. The hospital trains doctors and medical technicians as well as nurses; more than 300 students are enrolled in its Mary Aikenhead School of Nursing.

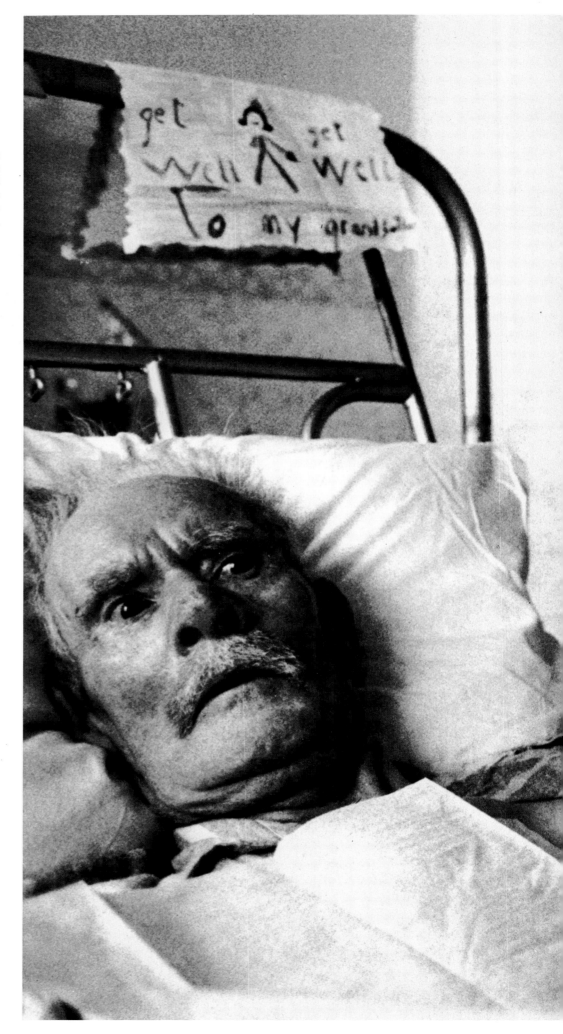

At one of the 20 or so Dublin campsites for Ireland's large itinerant population, children are collected for transport to a primary school run by the Sisters.

Having received a bath and a clean change of clothes, pupils at the Sisters' primary school for itinerant children learn about the origins of Christmas.

At Mount St. Anne's Convent—the central novitiate of the Irish Sisters of Charity—a Jesuit priest gives instruction in the principles of religious life.

Relaxing at the end of the day, a Sister employs a resourceful table-tennis style against a lobbing opponent.

A novice, whiling away the evening hours with a rendition of traditional folk tunes, plucks an Irish harp in the common room of Mount St. Anne's Convent.

Over tea at Mount St. Anne's, a novice talks to two postulants seeking admission to the Irish Sisters of Charity. A postulant must go through a six-month initiation period before entering her novitiate. After two years as a novice, she takes temporary vows. A further six years must then elapse before she is free to take her final vows.

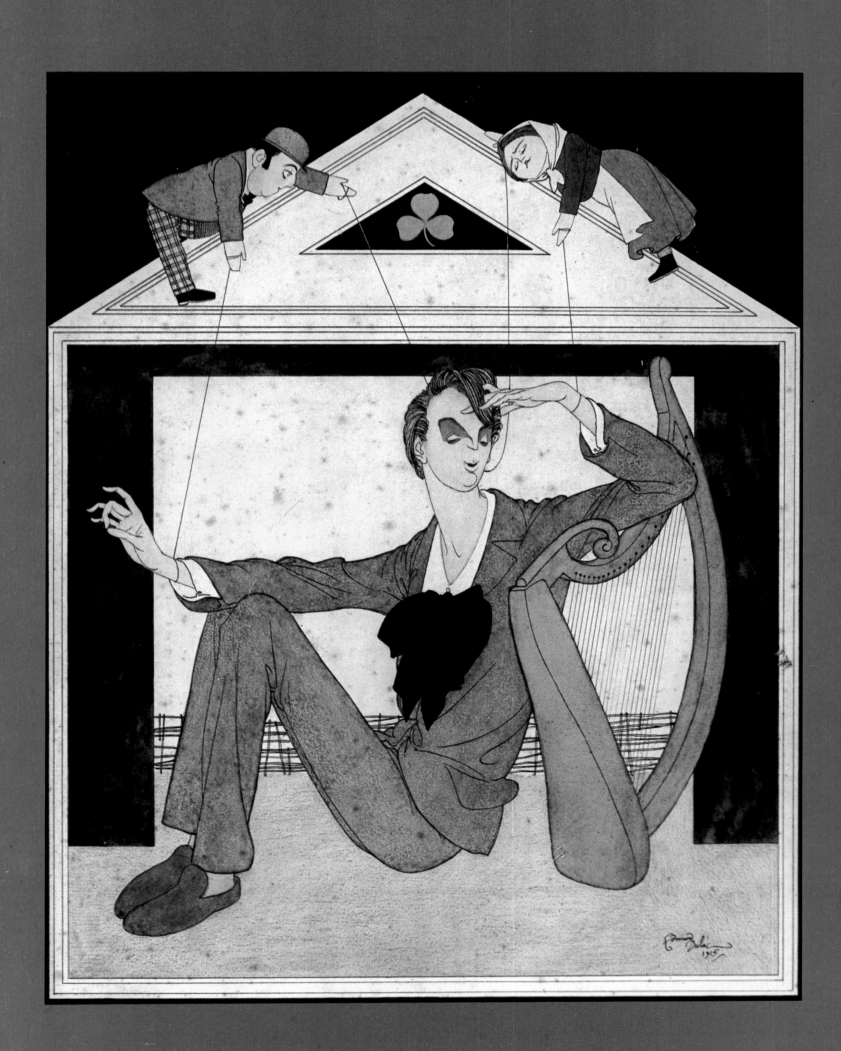

5

An Erratic Muse

The arts in Ireland are said to be blessed by the attentions of Kathleen ni Houlihan, who might be called muse, earth mother and national emblem rolled into one. The divine daughter of a legendary Celtic chieftain, she has become the personification of Ireland, gleaming through the mists of mythical prehistory to inspire poets and patriots alike. Weak, it is true, on serious music and not overly concerned with painting or sculpture, she has concentrated her favours on the word—sung, spoken and written—endowing Dublin with a tradition of literary excellence unsurpassed by cities ten times the size. In one remarkable 30-year period Irish Kathleen nurtured not only four of the world's finest playwrights—Oscar Wilde, Bernard Shaw, John Millington Synge and Sean O'Casey—but also the most revolutionary novelist of the 20th Century, James Joyce, and one of its greatest poets, William Butler Yeats.

Devotion to the word derives from an oral tradition of epic poetry and story-telling that flourished in Ireland for at least a thousand years before the arrival of Christian missionaries from Gaul and Britain in the 5th Century. At the centre of this ancient tradition was the *shanachie*, or professional poet, who was maintained at court or at public expense to entertain people with songs and sagas of Celtic heroes.

Even after the coming of Christianity and the cultivation of Gaelic as a written language, these Irish bards continued to roam the country, providing entertainment in return for food and a warm fireside. Held to possess magical as well as narrative powers, they rarely failed to receive a welcome. And on those occasions when hospitality or money was not readily forthcoming, they had a very effective way of showing their displeasure. One legend tells of a poet who wandered into Dublin in the hope of winning some sustenance from the local Gaelic-speaking Vikings. Finding himself ignored, the visitor is said to have struck fire from his harp and threatened the Vikings with that deadliest of all weapons in the Irish literary arsenal: satire. In those days it was believed that a man could actually die from a satire made against him, and the bard soon got his money.

It is still possible to detect relics of Celtic culture in the speech and writings of modern Dubliners, though the relics are no more than literary potsherds that have survived the ravages of time and colonization. The most obvious are the idioms carried across from the Gaelic, which 200 years ago was still the language of most of the people. The Gaelic word for "yes" has far fewer applications than its English equivalent, so the modern Dubliner might respond to the observation "He is a kind man"

Leaning on an Irish harp, an outsize puppet figure of William Butler Yeats spills out of a toy theatre in a 1915 caricature by the artist Edmund Dulac, who designed the costumes for one of Yeats's plays. Although he devoted his poetic genius to the cause of a resurgent Ireland, Yeats rejected the chauvinism of many Irish patriots—represented here by tiny puppeteers ineffectually pulling the strings.

with a recapitulation: "It's a kind man he surely is." Perfect tenses are scarcely used. "I'm after saying my prayers" is a more common form than "I have said . . . ." Two present tenses distinguish between habitual action —"I drink"—and specific acts—"I do be drinking". Gaelic lacks the personal pronoun "who" but manages to get by without it by use of present participles. So, for the most part, does the modern Dubliner. Instead of "I went up to Declan, who was drinking his Guinness", a Dubliner would be likelier to opt for ". . . Declan, and he gargling his stout".

It is when one tries to take a closer look at the thought behind the speech that the problems begin. I have neither the wit nor the wish to penetrate the Irishman's psyche, but occasionally I have the notion that it is diagrammatically laid out in some of the early medieval illuminated manuscripts that now repose in Trinity College Library or the Royal Irish Academy. The designs that are used on the pages often seem to be neither planned nor purposeful. Large introductory initials sway and curve and grow contorted appendages. Legibility is lost in a maze of whimsical doodles, scrolls and twirls, squiggles and coils, and interlaced patterns that resemble the weft and warp of fabric.

So, too, will the Irishman talk on—with easy digressions, and clauses and sub-clauses of digression—until the original purpose of his speech vanishes in a tangle of attractive irrelevance. Indeed, he has a wilful dislike of the plain and straightforward, and will avoid a direct question as if it were a booby trap. "What is the exact time?" you ask a Dublin police-man; and the classic reply is: "It is exactly between two and three."

Asking a Dubliner for street directions can produce a similar reaction. He is likely to tell you first one way *not* to go, then another, then perhaps another. Finally, he will describe a route both easier and a great deal shorter than your journey will eventually turn out to be. The intention is less to mislead than to please, and it stems, I think, from the old rules of hospitality that applied in a peasant society: the first duty was always to make the visitor feel good.

There may also be a vestige of the evasiveness employed by a suppressed people toward their masters. It was safer, during the years of English domination, for the Irishman to risk a reputation for inherent insanity by always twisting facts than to risk giving away information that might be turned against him. A century ago the English Poet Laureate, Alfred Lord Tennyson, spoke of "the blind hysterics of the Celt". In more recent times the English Catholic author, G. K. Chesterton, who professed admiration for the Irish, described them as "the men that God made mad". Both were expressing a view that many Englishmen have endorsed with more and less elegance of phrasing.

But if the exemplary Irishman is saner than he lets on, he is undeniably scatterbrained, with a proclivity to muddle and confusion, and an instinct for treading in mental quicksands that others are happier to avoid. (I

Emerging from a vortex of brilliantly coloured design, the Greek letters XPI—monogram for Christ's name—dominate a page of the Book of Kells, the most famous of Ireland's Celtic legacies. The book, which is now in the library of Trinity College, Dublin, contains the four gospels in Latin and is believed to have been produced in the late 8th Century by the monks of Iona, off the west coast of Scotland. When Norsemen invaded the area, the monks fled with their precious manuscript to the monastery of Kells, 35 miles north-west of Dublin.

bgeneramo

speak not of all Irish, nor even of the majority, but of a small quota whose traits are particularly striking, memorable or attractive.) Walking into an Irish tourist office one day to inquire about Dublin's next greyhound race-meeting, I was handed three different brochures on the subject. My pleasure at receiving such a bounty of information soon vanished, however, when I actually read the brochures and found that each one contradicted the other two.

The unique contortions of the Irish mind were vividly demonstrated for me by the waitress in a Grafton Street café. I had asked for a cup of coffee, price 20 pence. Sorry, she said; there was a minimum charge of 40 pence. Would I care for two cups? No, I replied; I'd have the apple pie. Sorry, but there were no tarts left. Perhaps I could have some cake, then? Sorry, but the baker had let them down fiercely that day. Well, could they give me a glass of wine? Now, wasn't that the awful thing— the café's licence hadn't yet arrived. Then came the dénouement to this perfectly good-humoured recital. The girl's eyes gleamed with the intensity of revelation: "Ye could have two small coffees. They're 15 pence each. That way ye'd only waste 10 pence."

Her suggestion was an unconscious echo of the insane logic that underlies that essentially Irish form of humour known as "the bull". (The origin of the word is unknown, but has to do with neither cattle rearing nor papal pronouncements.) Like the pun, the Irish bull makes a virtue of ineptitude, a joke out of sublime error. It commences from a wholly false premise and pursues the implications with a drive of sweet reason. A famous definition of the bull is itself an example of the genre: "The saying of a thing in an obscure way to make your meaning clearer than if you had put it in plain language." There are many such examples, but one of those I like best was recounted to me recently by an acquaintance who had been staying in a Dublin hotel. He was taking a bath one morning when a page-boy knocked on the door to deliver a letter. "Slide it under the door will you," said my friend. "Sure, I can *not*," replied the page-boy. "Isn't the letter on a tray?"

Among Dubliners it was Brian O'Nolan who most successfully raised the bull to the level of literature. Also writing under the pseudonyms of Flann O'Brien and Myles na Gopaleen, he was immensely prolific, publishing works in both English and Gaelic, and gassing the lunchtimes and evenings away in Dublin pubs till he died of cancer in 1966. Two of his techniques (if such a leaden term can be applied to will-o'-the-wisp genius) seem archetypically Irish. One was the marrying of whimsy with the language of the bureaucrat, the formality of a lawyer with the levity of a drunk, the pedantry of a schoolmaster with the twittering of a sparrow.

He writes demurely of a burp as "a coarse noise unassociated with the usages of gentlemen", then interpolates, with hectic change of mood, a string of oaths. He describes a hero of ancient Ireland in the solemn

This statue of the playwright George Bernard Shaw, erected near the National Gallery in 1966, is a more familiar part of the Dublin scene than Shaw ever was himself. At the age of 20 in 1876, he left the city where he was born and took up permanent residence in England. But in his irreverent wit and passion for controversy he always remained an intensely Irish author.

manner of the old sagas, but with an exaggeration that reduces the whole to the level of farce: "Three fifties of fosterlings could engage with handball against the wideness of his backside, which was wide enough to halt the march of warriors through a mountain pass." He puns outrageously: "The conclusion of your syllogism, I said lightly, is fallacious, being based on licensed premises." Of the alcoholic son of a titled gentleman he has one of his characters say: "There's a nip in the heir."

O'Nolan's other technique was to chart a course through shifting mirages of his own creation, all the while retaining a tenuous link with reality. This same technique is employed, of course, for the bull, but O'Nolan put it to much more ambitious and brilliant use in his novel, *At-Swim-Two-Birds*, in which—and the resumé, I should warn, calls for electric concentration—an author starting a novel creates such realistic characters that they come to life. The protagonist resigns all power over the creations of his own imagination and they, in turn, take over his life.

The fictional novelist finds one of his characters, a girl, so irresistible that he rapes her and, in doing so, begets a son. Later the son himself begins a novel in which his father, the author, is brought to trial for murder. Fictional events again become reality and the author's life seems in jeopardy until the chance burning of part of his original novel destroys the characters who are threatening him. Moreover, all that I have sketched takes place within yet another novel in which the narrator is trying to clarify his personal destiny. In spite of the tangles, and while cramming in more dimensions than are compatible with the laws of space and time, O'Nolan continuously, and by the exercise of a lunatic logic as keen as Toledo steel, commands our delighted attention.

Although no one has been more perceptive of the Dublin scene than the polyaliased O'Nolan, it was his friend and fellow writer, Brendan Behan, who came to dominate the scene itself. There has never been a Dubliner like him, before or since. In his ever-spreading frame he combined swashbuckler and aesthete, cynic and sentimentalist, braggart and weeper, dreamer and activist, blasphemer and believer, poet and jester.

Each of Behan's attitudes had a twist, for it was his habit to inflict hernias on orthodoxies of all kinds. He savaged the Church (which is conventional with Irish writers), but admitted that "blasphemy is the comic verse of belief". As a teenage member of the IRA, he tried to blow up British ships; but he had no time for the "earnest, religious-minded" revolutionary who took Holy Communion in the morning and committed murder in the afternoon. He was steadfastly loyal to his native town, but never missed the chance to swipe at its complacent conceits. "I like living in Dublin," he once said, "because all my enemies are about and it's very cosy."

Everyone has a story to tell of him because, in the 1940s and 1950s, everyone had seen something of him—holding forth in the pubs, lurching drunkenly about the streets, or prostrate in the gutter. The doctors warned

Shopping is temporarily forgotten as an old lady enters into spirited conversation with a passing friend.

Gift of the Gab

An admiring English observer once said of the Irish: "However commonplace may be the opinions which they express, these opinions are delivered with such a clarity of phrasing and such an astounding air of conviction that the dazzled visitor feels that the Oracle has spoken at last." Time has done nothing to diminish this Irish gift of the gab, and the average Dubliner loses few opportunities to display his mastery of the tall story or the telling phrase.

As this random but typical selection of Dublin street encounters shows, an afternoon walk can provide the vocal chords with as much exercise as the legs.

that alcohol would kill him, but nothing deterred his drinking—or his wit. One of the last remarks he made to the nun who nursed him during his final illness was: "May you live to be the mother of a bishop."

He died in 1964 and was given a Dublin funeral that a head of state might envy. Representatives of both the Irish government and the IRA paid their homage, and thousands lined the two-mile route to watch his coffin being carried from the Church of the Sacred Heart at Donnybrook to its final resting place at Glasnevin cemetery. "I know it is only foolishness in my own head," wrote Brian O'Nolan, "but there are streets in Dublin which seem strangely silent tonight. The noisy one-time son has gone home this time for good."

Part of the love for Behan came from his refusal to succumb to the sterling blandishments of London and New York. Except for rare, triumphal trips abroad (with interludes in jail or a hospital after drinking sprees) he never strayed far from Dublin—or Irish Kathleen. Not all of Kathleen's protégés have shown her such unwavering affection. The playwright Sean O'Casey was constrained to describe her, in terms that no Greek muse ever had to endure, as "an old snarly gob . . . an ignorant one too". And for James Joyce she was "the old sow that eats her farrow".

The trouble is that Kathleen tends to raise her votaries to the skies only to plunge them pell-mell to the bottom of the ocean, and Irish writers soon learn to be wary of their schizoid muse; for every truth about Ireland has a converse that is equally true. Cruelty is as specifically Irish as kindness, temper as tranquillity; and Dublin's conceit and philistinism are as characteristic of the place as artistic creativity.

Earlier this century Sir Hugh Lane, an Anglo-Irish philanthropist, wished to present the city with a superlative collection of paintings, including many French Impressionist works that he had the vision to value early. He also offered to house them in a building designed by Sir Edward Lutyens, one of the most distinguished English architects of the day. The Dublin city council met, deliberated, sniffed unhealthy foreign influences, bristled—and said no. Ireland's own artists, they asserted, could paint as well as any Frenchman.

As a result, when Lane went down with the *Lusitania* during the First World War, it was London's National Gallery that benefitted from his will. However, shortly before embarking on the *Lusitania*, he had left a codicil to his will stating that, if the Irish would build an art gallery, they could commandeer the pictures from London. But the codicil was unwitnessed and so the controversy over its provisions continued until the 1950s, when Dublin and London agreed to share the collection.

As J. M. Synge wrote in another connection: "I have the wildest admiration for the Irish peasants, and for Irishmen of known or unknown genius . . . but between the two there's an ungodly ruck of fat-faced, sweaty-headed swine." The grunts and rootings of this species have echoed on several notorious occasions. Two will serve as examples.

Brendan Behan (centre), whose drinking bouts won him almost as much fame as his plays, relaxes in a 1952 photograph taken at the family home in Dublin.

In 1907 one of the most moving and eloquent plays in the world's repertoire had its premiere at the Abbey Theatre in Dublin. It was Synge's *The Playboy of the Western World*. Concerned, in the main, with the admiring reactions of village girls to a honey-tongued braggart who claims, falsely, to have killed his domineering father, the play is truthful, tender, funny and at times the tiniest bit ribald. From the world it has evoked unstinting praise, loud laughter, long runs, film versions, myriad Ph.D. theses. From Dublin audiences it drew boos, catcalls, missiles and riots. In place of genius the Irish saw an assault on the purity of their womenfolk, a travesty of Catholic respectability and an affront to national honour.

One of the Abbey Theatre officials described the tumultuous first night: "There were free fights in the stalls . . . and at one time it seemed as if the stage would be stormed. It was lucky for themselves that the patriots did not venture as far as that, for our call-boy, who was also boiler attendant and general factotum, had armed himself with a big axe from the boiler-room, and swore by all the saints in the calendar that he would chop the head off the first lad who came over the footlights. And knowing him, I haven't a shadow of doubt that he would have chopped."

Nineteen years later history repeated itself. The play this time was Sean O'Casey's *The Plough and the Stars*. Again, it was a work of genius; and again the righteous indignation of the playgoers flared in a holy salvo of brickbats, this time on the fourth night. O'Casey had been treacherous enough to show that the slum-dwellers of north Dublin were not saints to a man (or worse, to a woman), and were motivated by drink, malice, cowardice and indolence as much as by God and Ireland. What caused particular outrage was the fact that one of O'Casey's characters was a prostitute. Although prostitutes were then a familiar enough sight in the streets, it was the first time that one of them had actually been brought into the glare of the Dublin footlights.

Bravely, the ageing Yeats, director of the Abbey, walked on to the stage that night and, when the tumult had died down, began a speech not so different from the one he had made after the furore over Synge. "You have disgraced yourselves again," he declared. "Is this to be an ever-recurring celebration of the arrival of Irish genius? Synge first and then O'Casey. The news of the happenings of the past few minutes will go from country to country. Dublin has once more rocked the cradle of genius."

They were salutary words, but they did not influence the verdict of the Dublin reviewers next morning. The work of "a guttersnipe from the slums," they said: "Sewage School drama"; "Dirt for dirt's sake." Disillusioned by subsequent rows with the Abbey management, O'Casey took up permanent residence in England, forbidding even the return of his remains to Ireland.

It is because of Kathleen's refusal to sustain what she has nurtured that so many of Dublin's best writers have been found, not in the real Dublin,

A motif of the legendary Queen Maeve hunting with an Irish wolfhound has adorned every programme and publication of the Abbey Theatre since its foundation in 1904. The design, chosen by W. B. Yeats, the Abbey's first director, symbolizes his ideal of a national theatre that would draw inspiration from Ireland's Celtic folklore.

but in abstractions of the city that they have carried to foreign parts. "Ireland is a place or state of repose," wrote the Dublin poet and playwright, Oliver St. John Gogarty, more than 40 years ago, "where souls suffer from the hope that the time will come when they may go abroad." And still the talent embarks at Dublin's quays: Samuel Beckett for Paris, Aidan Higgins for Germany, Edna O'Brien and Iris Murdoch for England, and many more. Indeed, a substantial part of the literature that is usually called English is only such in the sense that leaves grown, picked, dried and toasted in Assam become English tea.

Not all the exiles, of course, are motivated solely by the search for intellectual freedom. A condition diagnosed locally as "absence of spondulicks" also contributes to the exodus. Absence of spondulicks means lack of money and, while this condition is unique neither to Irishmen nor to writers, it is particularly rampant amongst Irish writers. The people of Dublin buy more books per capita than those of any city in the United States; but because Ireland itself is so small, fewer books are sold in the entire Republic than are sold in greater Boston, which has a population double that of Dublin. The Irish writer who wishes to find a profitable market for his wares therefore has little choice but to look beyond Ireland.

Whatever their reasons for leaving her, Kathleen tends to take a stern view of the exiles. Although she herself is often the culpable cause of their flight, this does not prevent her from shouting insults at their vanishing backs. They were not pure Irish anyway, she claims, ignoring the fact that there are no pure Irish. And if there is a particle of pure Irishness in them, she says with characteristic perversity, it will soon be corrupted by heathen foreign influences. One has only to look at the careers of two of her most brilliant protégés, Oscar Wilde and Bernard Shaw, to see how wrong she is. Both were lionized in England, but neither can be said to have betrayed their talent—or their Irishness.

The success of Wilde, for instance, who left Dublin for England in 1874 at the age of 20, was based on his knack of knocking down English totems in a way the English adored. No group in England repeats his description of fox-hunting—"the unspeakable in full pursuit of the uneatable"—as often as those who hunt. His remark on arrival in the United States for his first lecture tour—that he had nothing to declare but his genius—won immortality back in England, where self-advertisement was regarded as one of the worst of the social sins. Even in prison and disgrace for his homosexual activities, he could complain: "If this is the way Queen Victoria treats her convicts, she doesn't deserve to have any." And it was again with the endearing, calculated impertinence of the schoolboy that he announced: "The only way to get rid of a temptation is to yield to it."

Bernard Shaw, who also spotted the masochistic chink in English armour, achieved even greater success than Wilde. Shaw's impish wit and pugnacity enabled him to dominate London's West End for almost

Uproar at the Abbey

In a city famous for controversy, few incidents have sparked more furore than the Abbey Theatre's 1926 production of *The Plough and the Stars*. Its author, Sean O'Casey, dared to suggest that the heroes of the Easter Rising were ordinary mortals—fond of a drink, susceptible to a pretty face, even a little afraid to die. But the provocation was not purely political. The moralists were equally outraged that one of the play's characters, Rosie Redmond, was a prostitute.

The storm broke on the fourth night when critics descended on the Abbey in force. Patriotic banners were unfurled, vegetables, shoes and chairs were flung, and fighting broke out on the stage. Although the police eventually succeeded in restoring order to the theatre, O'Casey was reviled in the Irish press as "a guttersnipe from the slums" and a creator of "Sewage School drama".

A stage set for the original production of O'Casey's play represents a Dublin pub.

who will be

an Casey

21/ / /

During rehearsals Sean O'Casey mugs with Ria Mooney, who played the prostitute. "Be clever, my gal," O'Casey has scrawled, "& let who will be good."

three quarters of a century, and his plays have been seen by more theatre-goers than those of any English playwright since Shakespeare. Like Wilde, he also had a ready answer for any situation. To a heckler who shouted out that the production of his play *Arms and the Man* had been terrible, he replied: "I agree with you, sir, but who are we against so many?"

A plaque outside the University College student centre in St. Stephen's Green commemorates an ex-student who became the greatest of all Kathleen's prodigal sons. The plaque was not there when I first knew the city, nor was it thinkable that it ever should be. Joyce's great novel, *Ulysses*, which some rank in literature where Darwin's theory of evolution stands in biology, was never banned in Ireland for the simple reason that no one ever considered publishing or purveying a work that, for more than half a century after its appearance in Paris in 1922, was regarded as unalloyed pornography and a defamation of Dublin.

Now *Ulysses*, *A Portrait of the Artist as a Young Man*, and the collection of short stories known as *Dubliners* are, together with an ever-fattening corpus of critical works on Joyce, to the fore in every Dublin bookshop. He has become a major prop of the tourist industry, drawing academics from every campus in the United States to attend seminars, visit the Dublin he was so anxious to leave (but which he described with minute accuracy), and split every hair on his mouldering pate in an attempt to discover the ichor that flowed in his veins.

He left Dublin in 1904, after failing to find a publisher for *Dubliners*, and lived from then on in Rome, Trieste, Paris and Zurich, often in poverty, often in the gloom of the outlaw. His bitterness emerges in *Gas From a Burner*, a broadside of corrosively satirical verse that he privately published in 1912:

This lovely land that always sent
Her writers and artists to banishment
And in the spirit of Irish fun
Betrayed her own leaders, one by one.
'Twas Irish humour, wet and dry
Flung quicklime in Parnell's eye. . . .

He revisited Dublin only twice—the last occasion was in 1912—yet the Dublin he took away in his mind was more life-like than that of many who never left. Joyce himself claimed that, if ever the city were destroyed, it could be rebuilt, brick by brick, from his descriptions in *Ulysses*.

The book tells of a day in the life of the city—ostensibly June 15, 1904 —as seen through the eyes of a young teacher, Stephen Dedalus (based on Joyce himself), and of Leopold Bloom, an amiable and ineffectual Jewish advertising man with a randy and promiscuous wife, Molly. Long passages consist of minutely observed topography and recorded conversations of people Joyce had known. (Several, who became distinguished

The library at Trinity College, 270 feet long, was designed by Thomas Burgh, an Irish architect who gave 18th-Century Dublin many fine buildings. Founded in 1592 for "the reformation of the barbarism of this rude people", the mainly Protestant college has produced many distinguished men of letters, including Jonathan Swift, Oliver Goldsmith, Edmund Burke, Oscar Wilde and J. M. Synge.

in their own right, found to their annoyance that inclusion in the book brought them the widest fame.)

Ulysses delves into the sub-conscious, the intellect and the passions, probing some curious strata of sexuality. It also rings to the inescapable chiming of the Catholic Angelus bell. It is, in parts, infuriatingly obscure—obscurantist even. It has been described by one eminent Irish critic as "that immortal, unreadable work", and by another as having "the qualities of a powerful microscope directed on to the sediment of last week's milk bottle". Yet, at the same time, it offers such perceptive insights, such strange and revealing nuances, such mastery of words, rhythms and images that each impulse to throw the book aside—and they are many in my case—is annulled by some last-minute discovery of evident inspiration.

It so happened that, while the young Joyce was storing away images of Dublin for the years of exile, the city was experiencing an extraordinary cultural resurgence. The lodestar of the new movement was W. B. Yeats. Like Joyce, Yeats is a figure of endless complexity; like Joyce, he is also the subject of miles of dusty theses. No two figures, however, could be more different. Joyce kept to the truths he saw with the fidelity of a leech. Yeats started with a vision and tried to make it the truth. If *Ulysses* is not fit to read, Joyce could proclaim, life is not fit to live; *Ulysses* was life, or as much of that mercurial essence as can be caught on paper. But for Yeats, life was a second-rate process that needed to be validated by dreams.

Each solemn stage in Yeats's development has a comic side, though he tended to hide his own sharp wit behind a pompous exterior. Maud Gonne, the beautiful actress and fierce champion of Irish republicanism whom he wooed repeatedly and as often failed to win, summed him up nicely: "Willy was so silly." A prey to every zany fad an escapist age was able to fashion, Yeats loved art, ravens, lotus flowers, Byzantium and the occult. (What he did not love was old age, and Dublin wags nicknamed him "The Gland Old Man" because of his prodigious interest in surgical rejuvenation.) Everything that was opaque, ambivalent and cabalistic appealed to him. Although he was born in Dublin and educated in England, he spent much of his time among the remote hills of County Sligo, in the north-west of Ireland, where local legends about goblins and dragons, imps and fairies excited his imagination. And when, through Maude Gonne, he lit on the aspirations of Irish nationalists, he added an exciting dimension to their hopes by inspiring them with a faith in the supernatural destiny of the Celt.

From Yeats's cerebrations and infectious enthusiasm exploded a plan for a renaissance of the genius of Ireland. Art was to be an instrument for refining and transforming not merely the cultural but also the moral character of the nation. "To the great poets everything they see has its relation to the national life," he wrote, "and through that to the universal and divine life. . . . You can no more have the greater poetry without a nation than religion without symbols. One can only reach out to the universe with a gloved hand—that glove is one's nation, the only thing one knows even a little of."

Artistic manifestos almost invariably lead to a blossoming of the mediocre, but in Yeats's case the rule snapped. In 1899 he and his friends established in Dublin their Irish Literary Theatre (forerunner of the Abbey) and for a full decade the city was to be the most vital cultural centre in Europe. Without the achievement of those few years, the literary reputation of Dublin would be halved.

Yeats's movement dovetailed with more overtly political developments: the ill-fated attempt to revive the Gaelic tongue and the fumbling steps towards armed revolt. He flirted with the linguists and the gunmen. His ideal was to blend love of country—the Cult of the Celt—with the love, as he put it, of the Unseen Life—the Cult of the Divine—and he enriched the independence campaign with the symbolism of ancient heroes, investing it with a purer passion and a more poetic perception of Ireland's destiny. It was not Yeats's fault if that destiny was far too rich ever to be fulfilled.

Yeats's three principal lieutenants, all of whom, as it happened, belonged to land-owning gentry in the west of Ireland, made an ill-matched trio. Yeats himself supplied the vision and a tone of regal patronage. Lady Augusta Gregory, a gifted playwright whom O'Casey later described as looking like "an old, elegant nun of a new order", brought a strain of earthy realism and much stolid research into the tales and drama of the Irish peasants on which she based her plays.

Edward Martyn, the only Catholic in the group, contributed an understanding of some aesthetic trends in other lands, a passion for traditional church music and a penchant for provoking apoplexy among the upper echelons of Dublin society. (Having fought a long and expensive lawsuit against his expulsion from the ultra-conservative Kildare Street Club, Martyn is said to have knelt in the reading room, rosary beads in hand, and offered up appropriate devotions. When asked why he insisted on belonging to a club so hostile to him personally and so violently opposed to his political and religious beliefs, he replied: "It is the only place in Dublin where I can get caviare.")

The other member of the trio was the novelist George Moore, an irascible poseur whose extravagant iconoclasm led Yeats to call him "the Aristophanes of Ireland". His bumptiously egotistical three-volume memoirs, *Ave, Salve, Vale* (*Hail and Farewell*), show better than most literary reminiscences how impossible it is to reconcile the individual whims, caprices and aspirations of arty folk, much less force them into any kind of national glove. "I came to give Ireland back her language," Moore wrote later. The remark, coming from one who never tried to learn Gaelic and had skipped over to Paris as soon as his pockets were filled with the rents from his Irish estates, wanted conviction.

Just before exiling himself from Ireland in the summer of 1904, James Joyce (left) took up residence in the Sandycove Martello Tower (above), a 19th-Century fortification on the outskirts of Dublin. Writing "Ulysses" a decade later in Zurich, Joyce chose the tower as the setting for the novel's opening scene.

Running throughout the whole movement was a corresponding incompatibility of aim and realization. Yeats never learned that the common people of Dublin had turned their backs on the flowers, birds and romances of their rural sources; nor had they any wish to remember them other than in songs sung in bars, unsteadily and late at night. Yeats and his associates peered at their fellow-countrymen through the rosy tints of romanticism and bewailed "the fatal deterioration of the Celt" that followed from contact with the Saxon. But Dubliners thanked God for their release from the tyranny of the soil, noted that none of the leaders of the movement was short on Saxon blood, and mischievously allotted to Yeats's plays points for what they called P.Q.: Peasant Quality.

Artifice of aim was matched by maladroitness of method. What was virtually the inaugural play of the era—Yeats's *Countess Cathleen*, first performed in 1899—centred on the Faustian and somewhat condescending theme of a noble lady selling her soul to the Devil in order to save her humble peasant dependents. The pious Edward Martyn, having wrestled with his conscience over what he saw as the play's innate blasphemy, resigned from the movement, a gesture he was to repeat over a number of issues. Yeats recruited a priest to give his blessing to the play and Martyn climbed down. The respite was short-lived. Some Dubliners detected in the characterization of Cathleen a vilification of Irish womanhood and attempted—unsuccessfully on this occasion—to provoke a riot on the first night.

A year later Yeats and Moore, with naive optimism, decided to collaborate on a new play called *Diarmuid and Grainne*, which was based

A modern-day swimmer plunges into Forty Foot pool, the bathing spot used by Joyce and Oliver St. John Gogarty, the fellow-writer with whom Joyce stayed at Sandycove. Gogarty—who appears in "Ulysses" as the blasphemous Buck Mulligan—called Joyce "the scorner of mediocrity and scourge of the multitude".

on an ancient Celtic myth of love, elopement and tragic death. Closeted together, the two dramatists argued, raged and sulked—and eventually compromised. Moore wrote the play in French, in which he was fluent, after which it was translated by a Gaelic-speaking poet into Irish to give it the requisite P.Q. Lady Gregory then put the new form into an attractive Anglo-Irish dialect that was spoken near her home in County Galway, in the west of Ireland. Finally, Olympian Yeats adjusted points of style. It was not a recipe for immortality, and the play has sunk with little trace.

Nevertheless, the years that followed were ones of amazing achievement. The Abbey Theatre, founded in 1904, soon gained a world-wide reputation and survives thrivingly to this day. What came to distinguish it was not only the plays staged there but also the manner of their staging. Sets were sparse, movement was pared to a minimum and dialogue was chanted rather than spoken. These innovations reflected Yeats's view that poetical or legendary drama should have neither a realistic nor an elaborate setting, but one that was symbolic and unassertively decorative. "A forest, for instance," he wrote, "should be represented by a forest pattern and not a forest painting . . . The acting should have an equivalent distance to that of the play from common realities. The plays might be almost, in some cases, modern mystery plays."

One of the first and greatest of the Abbey productions was J. M. Synge's *Riders to the Sea*, a lyrical evocation of life in a small Irish fishing community. In 1898 Yeats had found Synge living disconsolately in Paris, then the obligatory residence for a young man dedicated to art. Yeats recognized in his fellow Dubliner "Aeschylus and Sophocles rolled into one" and recommended a move from bohemian Montparnasse to the bleak and misty Aran Islands, off the west coast of Ireland, where the life and language of the local fisherfolk had hardly changed in a thousand years. "Live there," urged Yeats, "as if you were one of the people themselves; express a life that has never found expression." Synge took the advice and in the short time that remained to him—he was to die of cancer in 1909, at the age of 38—wrote a series of masterpieces against which the jibes about P.Q. could find no hold.

The new cultural dynamism was by no means confined to the theatre. Edward Martyn instituted the annual Feis Ceoil, a festival of Irish music and dance that still continues in Dublin. He also founded the Palestrina Choir in the Pro-Cathedral, thus revealing the talents of one of Ireland's finest singers, John McCormack. Poems—many good—proliferated from young men like flowers in springtime. Books and magazines appeared on art, history, religion, mythology, politics, philosophy. There was a steady output of fiction. And talk flowed in torrents as the revivalist spirit spread, the subjects for decision multiplied, and the luminaries of the movement appropriated different evenings of the week for open At Homes.

One of the activists defined a literary movement as "five or six people who live in the same town and hate each other cordially". Certainly in this movement few were free from malice. Cracks of animosity opened and were patched, but the fabric could not hold together indefinitely. Everyone made fun of Moore, who asked for it with scurrilous bragging about his supposed rapes and romances. "Thou could'st tell many a pleasant tale of love," he once sang to his fireside rug in hostile company, earning a riposte that became the delight of his enemies: "Some men kiss and do not tell . . . George Moore told and did not kiss."

Moore's anti-clericalism also aroused hostility, particularly from Edward Martyn. The two of them, according to Yeats, were bound together by mutual contempt, and eventually Martyn stood by one of his resignations. Moore also fell out with Lady Gregory, and therefore with Yeats himself, who depended on her utterly. An important financial backer of the Abbey withdrew her support in 1910 when a performance—more through error than design—was staged on the day of King Edward VII's death.

The movement was also continually besieged from without by Dublin's redoubtable militia of Grundies. Neither the Catholic puritan nor the fanatical patriot—in many cases they were one and the same—was prepared to tolerate any shade of grey in the portrayal of Irish virtues, and their strident attacks undoubtedly discouraged thousands whose support Yeats had been hoping to win. Not surprisingly, the protestors received generous backing from the more vociferous sections of the Catholic press. One sanctimonious reporter, for example, described the band of brainwashed young prudes (including Patrick Pearse, martyr of the 1916 uprising), who yelled abuse at the first-night performance of

Yeats's *Countess Cathleen*, as "clean, sane, cultured young Irishmen" engaged in no more than a "manful protest".

Nor was an ally to be found in the opposite camp of the Anglo-Irish, at that time still the country's ruling élite. "What silly speeches your Celtic people have been making," the eminent historian William Lecky once told an affronted Lady Gregory. And John Pentland Mahaffy, the acerbic Provost of Trinity College (and Oscar Wilde's former tutor and patron), dismissed the attempt to reinstate the Irish language as "a return to the dark ages". Even James Joyce, who might have been expected to support an Irish cultural revival, satirized what Yeats called the Celtic Twilight as "the cultic twalette".

All the bickering, jibing and rioting, however, could not detract from the movement's achievements. Above the weeds and stones of a city festering in misery and faction, vacillating in its loyalties, stifling in its self-righteous pruderies, rose a flower which, as much as the architecture of the 18th Century, gave Dublin fame, respect and greatness. In creating something that was uniquely and unequivocally Irish, Yeats and his friends had helped to contribute to the momentous events of 1916.

For his poem about the Easter Rising, Yeats produced the oft-quoted lines:

All changed, changed utterly:

A terrible beauty is born.

Later he came to worry about the contribution the movement had made to the terrible violence that was also born. The mob was in control, he warned in 1922, when civil war broke out over the terms of the Anglo-Irish Treaty; and unless its reign was broken, Irish public life would relapse into more violence or mere apathy. Either way, Yeats foresaw that "our men of letters [will] live like outlaws in their own country". Unable to face the ugly outcome of so many golden hopes and dreams, he spent most of his remaining years in England, where he also wrote his finest poetry.

As it turned out, the violence gave way to an encroaching mediocrity, from which, with few exceptions, the best writers have continued to escape. Whatever may have changed, and changed utterly, it was certainly not Kathleen ni Houlihan.

Hard School of the Streets

PHOTOGRAPHS BY JOHN McDERMOTT

In the cobbled wilderness they regard as their private kingdom, youngsters of Dublin's backstreets confront intruders with a blend of shyness and defiance.

Away from the main thoroughfares, Dublin sometimes seems to be a city of children. The combination of large families (the birth rate averages more than 3.5 children per couple) and cramped housing conspires to make the grey backstreets of the metropolis a teeming playground where toddlers take their first steps, older boys or girls gather in impromptu gangs—and adults rarely seem to intrude. The streets even become a place of work for some children, who supplement their pocket money by selling trifles or by begging coins from passers-by. Whatever its uses, this realm of grimy cobbles and graffiti-stained walls has the look of a hard training-ground; yet the faces of its young inhabitants, combining innocence with worldly wisdom, suggest not so much the hardship of city life as the resilience and charm of Dubliners in the making.

Children demonstrate four variations of the Irish smile—from an impish grin to a full, gap-toothed guffaw.

Playing in the Liberties, one of Dublin's oldest areas, a young colleen displays the characteristic comeliness of her Irish lineage.

A girl earns money for the Christmas holidays by selling wrapping paper.

With a knee-level view of the passing parade of adults, a child on O'Connell Bridge, in the city centre, holds up a cardboard box and calls out for small change.

Content with their own company, three girls share a treat with a baby sister. Boys and girls on the city's streets seem to occupy separate worlds.

Taking a breather from a game played with an old broom, a boy lounges against a graffiti-covered wall while his friend keeps a dubious eye on a young intruder.

Forlorn young itinerants, children of Ireland's travelling tinkers, gaze questioningly at the passing world. Only about half of such youngsters go to school.

6

Diversions and Delights

Consider these symptoms. The contents of the skull are bound by an ever-tightening hoop of steel. A continuous monotone whine sounds in at least one ear. The muscles of the eyes are at full stretch, trying to hold open their lids. Somebody is talking, and attention is expected, a reply even. But thoughts, on their way from brain to lips to be articulated, are derailed by limpet mines. The distant wall distorts itself and closes in. Escape is impossible; neither foot would know the other's designs. People laugh and hoot maniacally.

This predicament is autobiographical, and it has nothing to do with the KGB, Smersh or any sort of third-degree session, with attendant extraction of finger-nails. It is something that has happened to me on more than one occasion in a Dublin pub, and it will doubtless happen again. It is the state I get into when, amid friends, song, wit and camaraderie, I down—over a period of a few hours—five or six cream-capped jars of dark stout. For me, it is an inferno to which, from time to time, I am consigned by social obligation. For many a Dubliner, it is paradise.

Drink is the sea on which Dublin's entertainment floats. Although statistics tell that the average Irishman drinks less than his English counterpart, this fact is deceptive. Owing to piety or doctors' orders, a large number of people drink no alcoholic liquors at all. The Sacred Heart lapel badge of the Pioneer Total Abstinence Association, a group that has sworn enmity to the bottle, is a more common sight than the circular brooch that proclaims a Gaelic speaker. But abstainers arouse suspicion among those outside the rule. "I would always recommend caution in dealings with an Irish teetotaller," said the waspish novelist Honor Tracy: "There was never a Pioneer but was a bastard at heart."

Despite the Irishman's high degree of godliness, pubs in Dublin are said to outnumber priests by two to one. In James Joyce's *Ulysses*, the protagonist Stephen Dedalus muses that it would be a challenging game to get from one side of the city to the other without passing the doors of a pub—and the situation is not far different today.

Every afternoon at 2.30, the bars close down by law and stay closed until 3.30. This interval is known as Holy Hour and can be recognized by the appearance of little knots of men, stretching out their last goodbyes on the doorsteps of the pubs, reluctant to end the elation of a lunch-time's hard drinking, hoping the hour will pass quickly so that it can all start again. And is that so unreasonable? The bar, after all, is the quintessential expression of Dublin delights, for it is the setting where drink and talk

Beside a board marked with the latest odds, a bookmaker at Shelbourne Park, one of Dublin's two greyhound tracks, hands a betting slip to one of his clients. Greyhound meetings, held at night, are becoming more popular every year and now compete with horse racing as the Dubliner's favoured way of redistributing his weekly wage.

blend into an alloy of unsurpassed congeniality. This blend has given rise to myths that, with the passing of time, grow more and more distant from reality. Many a visitor to Dublin enters a pub in the hope of hearing poets ad libbing timeless verse, or philosophers extracting eternal truths, like the sibylline prophet, from the fumes of their dark stout. Sad to say, however, the talk one overhears is often full of bourgeois innuendo, of bragging Mammon, of details of deals, houses, parties, cars.

Bars have changed in other ways. Although drinking remains a predominantly manly occupation, women—here as elsewhere—have invaded the bars and are adding, or causing to be added, a feminine touch to the décor that mightily offends the old-fashioned purist. In the last decade, the genteel lounge bar—a smart and titivated affair, baited with carpets, softer seats and other homely touches to lure the female drinker—has made impressive gains at the expense of yesteryear's bare drinking-chamber, where the floors were strewn with sawdust, the walls were yellowed by smoke and dappled by any jetsam of décor that the tide of history had deposited there, and talk and liquor could flow with uninhibited abandon. Still, the old-style bar is not dead. Walk any street in Dublin and you will soon detect a familiar reek emanating from some doorway: the mingled fumes of malt and urine.

Drunks are one of the sights that have become less familiar over the period I have known Dublin, but you still see them too: men and women, cursing, staggering, lurching, zig-zagging, mouthing obscenities at invisible enemies—betrayers, wives, husbands. In the vicinity of St. Stephen's Green, I have often passed a particular grey-haired woman with sun-bronzed skin and ragged tweeds, snoring on the pavement, smiling seraphically at some inward vision. And the unsteady baritone—warbling a ballad, or some over-exposed bel canto aria, or more likely a hit from one of the great American post-war musicals—is a familiar sound at the evening's close.

The drinking capacity of the Irish has always been a cause for comment by visitors. It is not confined to any class or race, though it had an extra significance for Dublin slum-dwellers, as that seasoned drinker, Brendan Behan, recalls in his memoirs of Dublin after the First World War. It was no social disgrace for the poor, he said, to be drunk. Getting enough to eat was regarded as an achievement, getting drunk something of a victory. Long before Behan's time, foreign travellers were noting the number of drunks in the streets of Dublin, the huge amounts they consumed before any outward sign was visible, and the colossal liberality of urban grandees and country squires towards their foreign guests. Claret and port were downed by the pint. Barmen developed the habit of breaking stems off glasses so that customers had to keep them in their hands and would therefore empty them quicker. When, after dinner among the gentry, the ladies retired, a porcelain-lined side cupboard was opened, and into it the gentlemen expended the excess liquid from their systems before proceeding to more serious and single-minded consumption. I have occasionally experienced the tail-end of this hard-drinking tradition and gone to bed with a turbine implanted in my brain; but each following morning, oblivion intercedes, so that I am likely to repeat the error. What I do remember from frequent observation is the sight and climate of many boat trips from Dublin to England: stacks of emptied bottles on tables, the offensive reek, faces progressing through white to pale green, bodies stretched on floor and couch and stair.

Dublin is founded on drink in more ways than one. Two of the biggest firms in the city are Guinness and Irish Distillers—the former brewing beers and stouts, the latter making Irish whiskey—and for more than a century they have made enormous contributions to the city's prosperity. Guinness, the stout, was an 18th-Century Irish invention, encouraged by a government aware of the ravages caused by harder spirits. Ireland's inventive claims cover not only the best of all stouts. Whiskey itself (spelt with an "e" in the Irish context, without it in the Scottish) is an Irish word, derived from the Gaelic *uisce beatha*, meaning the water of life, or aqua-vitae. The Scots are supposed, by the Irish anyway, to have adopted the Irish technique of distilling, dropping the "e" from the whiskey in the process. Even the drink's admirable foil, soda water, is alleged to have originated in Ireland, and there used to be a mineral well dispensing it in O'Connell Street. In his memoirs *As I Was Going Down Sackville Street*, written in the 1930s, Oliver St. John Gogarty described soda water as "a temperance drink, but . . . fated to be associated with whiskey until the end of time . . . perfect proof that not only is there a Providence, but that Providence disapproves of teetotallers".

The Guinness brewery remains in Dublin, distinguishing a large sector of the high ground on the city's south-west with its huge edifices and a large periphery of model housing for workers. (The housing was erected, on the initiative of successive Guinness chairmen, in place of some of the worst turn-of-the-century slums.) The Guinness empire has created an unusual Irish phenomenon: a family with a world-wide cachet—something like that attaching to Rothschild or Oppenheim—that is nevertheless totally at peace with the new Irish Establishment. There are innumerable Guinness charities, founded by stern family philanthropists of the 19th Century and continued to this day (as is often pointed out, in Dublin you can drink yourself into a state of benefaction: a percentage of every pint drunk goes to the relief of the poor). Guinness money has also financed, and continues to finance, pleasure parks, music festivals, university appointments and buildings, horse-racing and other sporting events. The Government's Department of Foreign Affairs is housed in a grand old Guinness mansion on St. Stephens Green, and the energies, as well as much money, of the Honourable Desmond Guinness, son of the firm's chairman, go to preserving some of the finer buildings of Georgian Ireland which might otherwise be lost through decay or demolition.

A favourite pub of mine, the Brazen Head, is itself a Georgian monument. Noted for its congenial decrepitude, it stands in the shadow of Christ Church Cathedral, surviving obstinately amid the windswept clearances recently effected in that area. The Brazen Head is Dublin's oldest bar. The nationalist rebel, Robert Emmet, drank there nearly two hundred years ago and plotted the rising that—snuffed almost before it was lit—earned him a speedy beheading outside St. Catherine's Church up the hill. It was a coaching house then, and you still reach it by way of a coach alley, although the entrance nowadays is flanked by a greengrocer and the Anna Liffia Beauty Salon. Within the crooked Georgian structure, which seems to be defying some fundamental physical laws in remaining standing, the bar itself is tucked away amid a warren of passages and is dimly lit. Shelves support a tangle and tumble of bottles and glasses, lamps, clutter and bric-à-brac that bespeak the magpie rather than the connoisseur—yet suggest a near-miraculous process of unconscious arrangement, a ferment from which the curlicued wizardry of ancient Celtic art was distilled.

An evening at the Brazen Head starts quietly. There are social creakings as the warmth of conversation begins to flow round the pipes.

"Hallo now, Kevin. Will it be a pint?"

"Terrible changeable weather it is so. Sure you wouldn't know which clothes to pawn."

"Oh indeed you wouldn't. You certainly would not."

"Fierce weather it is. There's no doubt of that."

There are few women, and those there are stand out like sightseers. For an hour or two you can hear the taped music from a loudspeaker behind the bar: Crosby, Sinatra and others, despite the notice "Only Traditional Irish Music allowed in this bar". But some time after nine, a murmuring is heard in one corner, followed by a silence. Then somebody, feigning reluctance, begins to hum, and soon slots words into his melody like the pieces of a jigsaw:

While going the road to sweet Athy
A stick in my hand and a drop in my eye. . . .
Dedah dedah, ha-hummmmm.

Late in the evening—I have seen it again and again all over Ireland— ballad-singing takes on the quality of a proof of virility. Women have no part in the ritual, are lying in all likelihood in bed storing up the com- plaints that will make them the absent butt of many jokes. The Irish hero is the man who stands among other men, feet firm, glass swaying in rhythm, myopic eyes fighting off the assaults of liquor, and sings in tune and steadily some familiar song with those twiddly musical ornaments that can sound like a muezzin summoning the faithful to prayer and that

A dominating industrial presence near the centre of Dublin, the Guinness brewery is the largest in Europe, producing more than four million pints of stout a day.

Two lunchtime drinkers stroll through the narrow coach alley that leads from Bridge Street to Dublin's oldest pub, the Brazen Head, established in 1666. Located in an area of extensive redevelopment, it has survived with the aid of a listing in the City Corporation's register of protected buildings.

must go back to the Celtic, if not the Indo-European, dawn. A love-song it may be, but there is no woman here to win or woo:

Sure I spied a little miss
And I kindly asked her this
May I wind up your little ball of yarn?

It may be a dirge, with the eyes of the singer a spring of tears. But I find it hard to believe the emotion has anything to do with disappointed love. More likely it is nostalgia for a time, years ago, when the voice was in better trim and the body more erect, and the vocal fantasy nearer the possible:

Now I took her to a grove
Beneath a shady green
With no intention of doing her harm.

Writing has the force of the confessional. I have never till now related, nor even remembered, the shame I felt one evening in a bar close to Dublin two hours after the nominal closing hour—a time when lights are low and a ritual look-out is posted to watch for the authorities. A burly balladeer, the black hair of his chest matted up to his chin, asked me for a song. It is not that I lack a voice or some knowledge of Irish airs; I am quite capable of rendering *Danny Boy, Molly Malone, The Wearing of the Green,* or *The Foggy Dew.* But at that moment, nerves blotted out memory of all songs save *Speed Bonny Boat,* which seemed altogether too Scottish, jejune and hackneyed. So I refused, not once but many times, feeling, as we used to say at school, wet to the point of overflow; until he turned away with a sneer—I can still see the strong Roman nose turning into profile—as he might from some weedy fellow who refused his challenge to a fight. That, I suppose, as much as anything, revealed to me the Irishman's attitude to song which, like many of his other entertainments—and even his conversation—has a strong element of competition, bravado and display. It is like a courtship ritual whose detachment from its original purpose only strengthens the need to shine.

But there are other sides to singing. The pell-mell prattle of the Dubliner flows easily into song as his memory, searching an infinite store of traditional lyrics, finds a ballad to suit his mood. None, perhaps, are aired as frequently as the stories of martyrs and rebels, a custom that, exasperatingly to the regular English visitor if only quaintly to the first-time tourist, keeps alive the belief in an English Gestapo. In these songs, patriots hang in sight of their loved ones, English troops pike, lynch, rape and loot, flower-of-youth rebels bless their mothers with a final breath before the noose chokes them; and there is no shortage of brave little Irish bands that trounce regiments of English soldiers and posses of police. Blessedly, sadness can change in a trice to comedy, to a picture of the races, to a marching song, to a game of football, a meaningless recital of verbal high jinks like the original *Finnegan's Wake,* or a jolly piece of bawdy innuendo:

In walked her husband and great was his shock
To find the blonde German had wound his wife's clock.

It is not only at the Brazen Head that people sing. The last decade or so has seen, as a kind of balance to the spread of leatherette, vinyl veneers and carbonated ales, a massive revival of folk song. Singing bars are found all over the town, and though Dubliners are quick to recognize a tourist draw when they see one, it is predominantly to native taste that they cater. Entertainment varies from set performances of songs and dances by visiting folk-groups to spontaneous ballad sessions begun and maintained by regulars. To some extent the revival is international. Well-known groups from overseas are hired by some pubs, between fixtures in grander venues, to sing their plangent laments about Vietnam or Mrs. Robinson or nuclear waste. In the main, however, bar songs are native produce. Indeed, some groups that began in bars—the Dubliners, the Clancy Brothers, the Chieftains—have themselves graduated to international limelight and successfully export huge repertoires to England, Europe and America.

I once heard a theory, which appealed to me strongly, that each human being is born, and spends his whole life, at the same age. (On these grounds I suspect I was born aged 43, and will shortly be dovetailing my spiritual with my technical age in what I hope will be a most fulfilling synthesis.) If the theory is turned to pubs, it seems obvious that Dublin's were best suited to the times, characters, attitudes and habits of the city during the 1930s, 40s, and 50s. Of course, it is hard to be sure that the young man you overhear in a pub pontificating about the demise of the novel and exuding, almost as a token of authority, a musty reek of body juices, is not an embryonic Behan or O'Nolan—to name just two geniuses of the day. It is easy to retain an exaggerated picture of yesteryear's snows, and the story is told that Behan and O'Nolan themselves were once overheard lamenting the disappearance of the Dublin "character".

All the same, those must have been, on any account, great times for the bars, when you might walk into McDaid's off Grafton Street and be sure of hobnobbing with poets, or the Pearl or Palace—both near the *Irish Times* building in Fleet Street—to be among journalists, or Madigan's off O'Connell Street to meet broadcasters and actors. And in the course of the pub crawl, you had a good chance of being treated to an *ad hoc* performance by the sharp-tongued poet Patrick Kavanagh, who when some bruised enemy of his told him, "You're only a minor poet after all", replied, after a magisterial pause, "Since Homer, we all are"; or by Behan, who in one pub began a sentence about Dublin's jail facilities, half-way through vomited copiously on the floor, and finally sat up and finished the sentence; or by Brian O'Nolan, who might be explaining why home-brewed poteen was an infallible cure for influenza—it rendered the virus itself drunk and incapable. (Later, on his deathbed in hospital,

O'Nolan snapped at a friend pouring him a last tumbler of gin and topping up with a thimble of tonic: "Don't drown it, you fool.")

In the era before Behan's, though pubs abounded, Dublin's cultural stars tended to entertain in private. True, the age of Yeats saw the great days of the Bailey, a pub in Duke Street where politicians and pioneers of the literary revival gathered in a room upstairs to while away their evenings in competitive displays of wit and erudition. But most entertaining went on at home, and there was then a recognized class of "bun-men" who preferred cafés like Bewley's on Grafton Street, where talk went on in a setting of red plush and cosy cubicles, without the stimulus of alcohol. Yeats himself made only one visit to a pub, accompanied by a poetic friend and cicerone. He sat at a table and ordered a sherry and when he had finished it stood up and said: "I have seen a pub now. Will you kindly take me home?" stepping into the brougham outside with evident relief.

Today the Bailey, like so many others, is soullessly smart; perhaps worse, it preserves in the lobby, as a misleading come-hither to culture seekers, the door of the now demolished No. 7 Eccles Street, model of the home of Leopold Bloom in *Ulysses*. It has in its time (though not under the present management) turned away a poet for wearing a hat and a well-known publisher for not wearing a tie. McDaid's regulars on the other hand seem a little too conscious of their heritage. One suspects that aspirant poets in their scarves, denim coats and rakishly angled caps over unkempt hair are wearing a uniform that can easily be slipped on after work, not the sum total of a seedy wardrobe. There is talk—I suppose there always has been, though the jargon was not so blandly psychological —of relationships ("I'm lucky," says a girl. "Ending a physical involvement always seems to leave the man more emotionally drained than myself.") and of parties, late hours and notable consumptions of drink: "Jasus, didn't I surround a whole bottle of whiskey last night?"

But drink remains a sure link with the past: the timeless tipping of the glass of whiskey, crossing the eyes to see the golden liquor flow slowly throatwards; and the long-drawn extraction of Guinness from the taps, creating a ritual like the tea ceremony of the Japanese, and spreading a topping of cream through which, in quest of transcendence, lips and tongue dip down to the savour of brown malt.

Of all the pleasures that alcohol lubricates, none is as widespread in Dublin as that team of temptresses, horses and the gambling they give rise to. Until quite recently, the horse was a necessity to Dubliners as well as a source of sport: right through the 1950s, horsedrawn carts rattled over cobbled roads and bridges conveying coal, beer barrels, various comestibles and the eclectic pickings of the gipsies. Now, although people in the west of the country still drive to church in traps (leaving their cars in the garage for God's day), horses are a rarity in Dublin's streets.

But in certain select quarters—the auction paddocks and spacious grounds of the Royal Dublin Society during the Spring Show and the August Horse Show, and throughout the year at the city's two racing tracks—the animals are a powerful motive force in the life of the locals, as of the entire nation. When a dozen or so yearlings or fillies line up under their midget riders in a windy corner of Phoenix Park or Leopardstown, men and women up and down the country are placing their last wagers in the crowded betting-shops, or hurrying to a telephone, or calling on their local bookmaker, pledging savings, shirts, beds, holidays, larders. An oceanic surge of people crowds the bookies on the course, to bet a pound, two, five, any denomination up to a thousand or more, in a continuous redistribution of the national income.

Behind these economics of frailty are the firmer facts of the horse industry. A combination of climate, soil, grass, bloodstock and a national passion for the animal transcending class and wealth causes the breeding of horses to be done better in Ireland than anywhere else in the world. From the peasant in County Mayo whose nag doubles as turf-hauler and beach-racer, to the millionaire breeders of County Kildare with green sward like velvet and a disinfected cleanliness pervading their shining white stables, Irishmen have horses in their blood.

The Irish invented steeplechasing and possibly modern show-jumping, introduced betting-shops in 1926—a good 35 years before the English had them—and helped mould polo, the sport of kings. They still convert their market towns periodically into horse-fairs—huge gatherings where horses of all descriptions are bought and sold—tethering the beasts to lampposts, garden gates and any available fixtures, and are so at home with their animals that, in the words of the 19th-Century humorists, Edith Somerville and Martin Ross: "if they have no convanient way to sit on the saddle they'll ride the neck o' the horse till such time as they gets an occasion to lave it." More than half the racehorses in Britain are Irish products, and a considerable percentage of those in America, France and elsewhere. Irish horses like Prince Regent, Golden Miller, Sheila's Cottage, Devon Loch, L'Escargot, Nicholas Silver, Arkle, Captain Christy, Rheingold and Levmoss are firmly established in the Turf's Hall of Fame.

The finances of the business match the achievement. An Irish stallion can earn three-quarters of a million pounds in stud fees in a single year, and may change hands for ten times that amount. Even non-thoroughbred show horses may fetch hundreds of thousands of pounds, and together with hunters, riding horses and sundry breeds of pony, collectively draw in several million pounds a year—increasingly these days from Arab states that, three hundred years ago, supplied the Ham, Shem and Japhet of all modern racing breeds.

No wonder, then, that Dubliners throughout the year obey the urge to take bus and car to their own courses, or those a few dozen miles out,

A retired priest is caught up in the drama of a soccer match between two great rivals, Cork Celtic and Shamrock Rovers, one of Dublin's five professional teams. His green-and-white scarf marks him as a Shamrock supporter.

like Naas and the Curragh in County Kildare. All are well set in the landscape—Leopardstown and Naas, in particular. There, the white railings stand out. against a gentle background of smooth hills, tufts of woods, and lines of hedge and horizon forming a study in linear greens. In your imagination you can people these scenes with Conchobar and his Red Knights or the noble Cuchulain—semi-mythic Celtic heroes who probably staged their own racing contests in sites that, give or take a concrete stand and a sea of cars, were just like these.

At the races, the comet of wealth glances against the planet of mere mortals with no offence for once to either—though Anglo-Irish features prevail in the Stewards' Enclosure, so that you can see where much of the money remains. The roll-call of racegoers includes old gipsy women at the gates selling spit-polished apples from dilapidated prams; rustics in heavy greatcoats of unspecifiable darkness, concealing keen sensitivity behind their bloodshot eyes; priests in black, maintaining a pastoral pose in the face of their own and others' weakness for the game of chance; a little old woman with the Parkinson shakes trying to read the odds in her newspaper while a little boy looks on with undisguised curiosity. Gathered around the bookmakers' stands are thin men with guilty, furtive, desperate looks, fat men with greasy complexions, fur-collared suede coats and cigars like totem poles, ordinary men and women you would never glance at twice. As the notes fall like confetti into the bookies' capacious leather cases, many a promise to wife or children or oneself is consigned to oblivion, and somewhere the computer of destiny enters a future visit of the bailiff, hours of sorrow-hedging in the pub, and a score more premature admissions to the hospital wards.

"Good jumper is it?" says a man near the bookies' stands. "Don't they have to tell the Air Traffic Control whenever he's running." There must be 50 or so bookies, their stands forming a rectangular palisade, connected by impalpable wires of high tension. The tick-tack man relays information between the stable, the odds board and the bookies by a kind of semaphore, gesticulating like a madman or a hideously flea-plagued chimpanzee, alternating these manic phases with periods of pious fallow, hands joined demurely in front. "Three minutes to go," warns the loudspeaker, and among the crowd the fever is on. The grandstand, deserted till now, fills like a beach at high tide, but the bets go on till the start and after. "Two pounds on Maid of May"; "I'll lay two to one the field" (meaning the favourite); "Take two and a half to one". At this stage, a rapt awe that even God might envy has descended on the course, and on all the souls throughout Ireland with something at stake.

After the start, which is furlongs away, little sound. A shout or two: "C'mon ye boy, ye." And a few more as the field approaches for the first time, but you can hear the hoof-thuds, breathing and motion, that unique package of muffled sound as they lollop up for the first time, clearing

A Dublin player makes a break for goal during an All-Ireland Hurling Grand Prix at Croke Park in the northern suburbs of the city. Hurling, a game unique to Ireland, is played with a heavy stick and a tiny, hard ball that can be struck, thrown or kicked. Enthusiasts claim it is the fastest game in the world.

hurdles in their stride, nine fleet horses whose takings in this national ballyhoo will be a pat on the neck and a bag of grain—or a bullet between the eyes if they muff a jump and break a bone. They pass, foaming at mouth and vent, satin coats runnelled by sweat, panting hard, while their riders' bottoms career like banners over the saddles intended for them; eyes forward in a circular route that gets them nowhere, but knits and breaks fortunes and keeps the bookies prospering.

On the final lap, excitement and decibels mount, but there are too many nerves at play for the full exercise of Irish wit and turn of phrase. That will come later: "Sure he was tannin' the hide off her behind; that way he wouldn't blind her"; "Jasus t'wasn't the fall hurt him; t'was the sudden stop". Now it's "C'mon Maid of May", "C'mon Pearly Gates", and another two thousand hearts leaping in silence. A small crescendo as the horses approach the second time. Then it's briskly over. A few people, suppressing their elation, collect winnings with shifty looks. The rest hope for better luck next time. And many, too young to know their own intransigent Irish natures, swear this time will be the last.

For some Dubliners, the appeal of racing pales beside that of more participatory sports. Considering the size of the city, there is an astonishing number of these. Each of the two English staples—often summed up as "soccer, a gentlemen's game played by hooligans, and rugger, a hooligans' game played by gentlemen"—commands large and loyal followings. Soccer, traditionally, is the native Dublinman's game: as in England, it is

Players leap to punch the ball during a Gaelic football match. A unique mixture of soccer and rugby, this Irish summer sport is faster than either—even injuries are not allowed to hold up play—and has fewer rules.

primarily a working-class sport. Rugby is pitched socially higher, among the middle class (not so long ago, it was exclusively Anglo-Irish). All but one of the city's 12 rugby grounds are situated in the more prosperous part of the city south of the Liffey, and several have social clubs where blazers, cravats and loud English accents are prominent.

Dublin contains a third sporting allegiance, scarcely found in England. Side by side with the triumph of political nationalism over the last century went a resurgence of Gaelic games—in particular, Gaelic football, hurling, handball and camogie. The native brand of football has similarities to rugby: there are 15 men to a side; the ball is propelled by hands as well as feet; and the goal-post is shaped like an "H". Hurling, played with a broad stick curved at the lower end, has affinities to hockey. Camogie is hurling adapted for women, mainly by the use of a lighter stick. Handball, played in a walled court, resembles Spanish pelota and English fives. All have a long history in Ireland, but none rivals hurling in antiquity.

Hurling is mentioned in a medieval account of Irish affairs more than a thousand years before Christ. Another annal of Celtic times records that, in the 2nd Century B.C., a dumb boy's speech was restored when he was hit on the shin with a hurling stick. His first words have not survived, which may be just as well, but he grew up to become a king. By the 14th Century A.D., English statutes were forbidding settlers in Ireland to play the game, on the grounds that their enjoyment of it prevented more martial exercises. Then, when Irish nationalist fever was running high in the final years of the last century, the Gaelic Athletic Association was founded to revive recreations which had been all but swamped by English innovations. Under the vigorous patronage of the GAA—and with encouragement from nationalist politicians, the Catholic Church, and organizations throughout the country—the sports quickly began to flourish.

The enthusiasm survives—and so does its patriotic element, with a concurrent Anglophobia. Up to 1971, the so-called Ban Rules, introduced in 1904, prevented any player, supporter or spectator of rugby, soccer, cricket or hockey from joining the GAA; and the ban still applies to all members of the British armed forces and police, of whom there are many thousands in Northern Ireland. Conversely, skill in Irish games can be an asset in an Irish political or business career. To understand why, one has only to attend any modern All-Ireland final, either of hurling or Gaelic football. These games take place at Croke Park in north Dublin, the GAA's headquarters and the largest sports stadium in the country. As many as a hundred thousand supporters crowd the huge stands, the colours of their teams fluttering on scarves, flags, hats and rosettes. For two hours or so, the vocal enthusiasm ebbs and flows across the ground and neighbouring suburbs, while the heroes of a generation are made and unmade on the field. The evening becomes a great one for the bars, and the next day's newspapers relegate the weightiest world news to insignificance.

At the National Ballroom in Parnell Square, a young man assesses a row of hopefuls. Despite the fashion elsewhere for discos, bistros and basement dives, this Dublin dance-hall, with its live bands and old-fashioned roominess, remains as popular as ever with teenagers on Saturday nights.

All of this is not to suggest that Dubliners in search of recreation invariably head for football fields or racecourses and finish up the day with a glass in hand. To paint Dublin as a city full of sports-mad pub-goers would be no more accurate than to portray the English as a regiment of stock-brokers with stiff upper lips and rolled umbrellas.

There are, and always were, connoisseurs in Dublin pursuing the good, the true and the beautiful, relishing their porcelain and Georgian Waterford crystal and 18th-Century Dublin silver under the rococo plasterwork of drawing rooms in Fitzwilliam Square and Merrion Square, passing their leisure in waspish displays of donnish wit, never approaching a racecourse or mere jar of stout. Every day, ladies of immaculate discernment are fitted for evening gowns on the premises of such voguish designers as Ib Jorgensen in Molesworth Street or Sybil Connolly in Merrion Square. At the National Gallery, lectures are delivered by plump professors and curly-haired young aesthetes who would recognize in what I have written almost nothing of the Dublin they know, have always known, and which has more than anything moulded their taste and delight in the subtle intricacies of oil, watercolour, stipple and impasto.

There are, in addition, theatre buffs whose appetites are well satisfied by the repertoires of half a dozen central theatres and a few more in the outskirts. There are men whose pleasure it is to spend hours among the sandy tussocks of the Bull, a wild promontory curving like a lobster claw round the mouth of Dublin harbour, to watch the estuary birds and record the grasses for which it is famous. Doubtless the curtains of the evening conceal many a stamp-collector checking through his collection, many a fitness fanatic straining through his press-ups, music-lovers playing music, chess-lovers playing chess, lovers pure and simple playing the games they love, not to mention the half million or so who will be watching the televised offerings of Telefis Eireann—the sole national network—or more likely those of the BBC, hooked in from the higher ether by their spindly aerials.

And then there are the young, and their brazen playground on the north side—O'Connell Street, Parnell Square and their purlieus. One of the great contrasts of Dublin is to pass from O'Connell Bridge to its wide and windy eponymous street. On the bridge, ragged, smear-faced itinerants, women with babes at their breasts, children with wild eyes and matted hair, sit or lie on the cold hard pavements, looking away from the dropped coins, passively anticipating an undernourished, sub-human life that sociologists show will last on average less than 40 years. Half a mile upstream you can glimpse an enchanting skyline of steeples, spires and Byzantine domes above the controversial Wood Quay, an area the Dublin Corporation threatens to choke with concrete office blocks. God's city, with Mammon at the gates. To me the view in the frost-clear twilight, a red sky behind, with its message of many faiths and much antiquity, is one of the greatest in Europe.

Yet there, at your elbow, is O'Connell Street, a wide and flashy thoroughfare, more hick-town than Irish. In the evenings, it is the resort of the young and unattached. Wind slews round from the river and whistles harshly up the street, disturbing the hair-dos of girls waiting for their lads outside the General Post Office, chilling the central cordon of statues: O'Connell, massive in bronze, towering hugely over the more life-size figures of heroines and angels; William Smith O'Brien, who led a disastrous rising in 1848; Parnell; the 19th-Century temperance leader, Father Mathew. Buildings still raw from their hurried construction after the Troubles 60 years ago house the features of a debased, third-hand American culture: amusement arcades, burger-bars, and arena-sized cafés selling fried potatoes and chicken under the spurious image of some Kentucky patriarch.

Several men click cameras at passers-by and hand them cards, and the willingness of many young people to be caught, here and now, on film, seems to underline the fleeting nature of this stage in their lives. O'Connell Street represents a short eruption of romance in workaday lives. It offers dance-halls and snack-bars to meet in, shooting-galleries and poolrooms to bring out manliness, chocolates and films to woo with, ring-shops to usher in the terminal contract. Everywhere there is music or muzak, synthetic melodies programmed to touch vulnerable emotions like steel on a raw wound, facilitating the holding of hands, the looking of looks, the meeting of lips. Even the Irish, with their inestimable gift for small-time chatter, need active solvents to dilute their shyness, as boys from garages and schools and banks eye the wallflowers at Conarchy's or Barry's dance parlours—nurses from the Maternity Hospital or students from local colleges or hostel-dwellers from Mountjoy Square—and pluck up courage to ask for a dance.

There are many incongruities in O'Connell Street: the grandiose sculptures, a waxen Christ encased in glass on a plinth; a stocky, bald evangelist with a face like Santa Claus's shouting his message of salvation against the drone of the traffic: "I say to you friends, that here, today, there is the glorious saviour Christ, who on that hill in Calvary paid with his life for all our sins. . . ." And there are the wagtails, black and white birds that have wintered in a huge flock among the central plane trees for as long as anyone can remember, regardless of the razzmatazz and the curious whine of the buses and the endless passing of cars and people. I often used to watch them in the bare branches, each in a constant fidget to find the fulcrum between its body and that long spatula of a tail. Occasionally one would fly quickly to the next tree, its white belly lit momentarily by the street lamps below. Why that bird, and why to the next tree were unanswerable questions.

But I have wondered whether the bird's move ever proved as momentous, as it unruffled its feathers beside new neighbours, as that of the lad who a few yards away was crossing the floor of Barry's, to ask another sort of bird to share the next dance, and perhaps the next; and then to buy a soft drink, and later perhaps a vodka in the Parnell Mooney's or Granby Bar; and a week or two later, on the back seat of his da's car, to kiss and fondle; and a few months afterwards, to pop the question that O'Connell Street, with its lights and chords and dazzle of moving colours, had been prodding him to ask; and finally, some months after that, to call out his and her relations in their dark, becoming suits, their toiles and crêpes and hats of raffia with plastic Easter roses attached, to watch her pledge her life to him and him his life to her before leaving the limelight to new generations, moving into some murky suburb and a whirlpool of mortgage and gas bills, with only one fading photograph, taken by a working photographer under the pillars of the GPO, to bring back the good times of their youth.

Where the Booze and Blarney Flow

PHOTOGRAPHS BY LAURIE LEWIS

In the International Bar, on Wicklow Street, two lunchtime drinkers exchange confidences over glasses of whiskey—an Irish invention, or so the Irish say.

"The whole profit of the towne stands upon alehouses," an Englishman wrote of Dublin in 1610. The observation may not have been literally true, but the capacity of the Irish for strong drink and good talk remains legendary. Dublin's pubs still provide a focus for the city's social life and favourite pastimes, from reading newspapers to listening to folk music. Older *habitués* may complain that too many pubs have been wantonly modernized, and that the fabled time earlier this century, when Dublin's intellectuals bandied wisecracks and eternal truths over glasses of stout, are forever gone. Yet a bevy of bars with fine Irish names like Doheny & Nesbitt's, Kavanagh's or O'Donoghue's still retain a simple, traditional atmosphere in which the shades of such celebrated literary tipplers as Brendan Behan or James Joyce would not feel out of place.

In Doheny & Nesbitt's, on Lower Baggot Street, a gentleman reads his paper in one of the cubicles provided for patrons who prefer to drink in relative privacy.

A mother and daughter chat in a secluded nook. Women tend to prefer a private booth to the crowded area around the bar, which is typically a male preserve.

A six-year-old sits with three young people in a bar. By law, only the proprietor's own children are allowed inside a pub—but the rule is widely ignored.

In James Gill's, on the North Circular Road, a street trader relaxes after work with one of the 60,000 pints of Guinness consumed in Dublin every day.

In Kavanagh's, a workmen's pub near the famous Glasnevin cemetery, two dedicated clients enjoy Ireland's national drink: a pint of stout drawn from the tap.

A genial barman at the Brazen Head swaps gossip with some of the regulars. James Joyce, who knew the pub well, immortalized it with a reference in "Ulysses".

A group of musicians playing accordions and fiddles provides free entertainment in O'Donoghue's, one of the most popular of Dublin's many "singing" pubs.

As closing time is called at Kavanagh's, a trio of solemn-faced regulars concentrate on matters of consequence—in all likelihood, the next day's racing form.

Bibliography

Caulfield, Max, *The Easter Rebellion.* Frederick Muller Ltd., London, 1964.
Clarke, Austin, *Twice Round The Black Church.* Routledge & Kegan Paul, London, 1962.
Clarke, Desmond, *Dublin.* B. T. Batsford Ltd., London, 1977.
Connery, Donald S., *The Irish.* Eyre and Spottiswoode, London, 1968.
Craig, Maurice, *Dublin 1660-1860.* Allen Figgis Ltd., Dublin, 1969.
Curran, C. P., *Dublin Decorative Plasterwork of the eighteenth and nineteenth Centuries.* Tiranti, London, 1969.
Dangerfield, George, *The Damnable Question.* Constable, London, 1977.
Dublin Tourism, *Dublin: Useful Information.* Dublin, 1977.
Ellmann, Richard, *James Joyce.* Oxford University Press, New York, 1959.
Ervine, St. John, *Bernard Shaw: His Life, Work and Friends.* Constable & Company Ltd., London, 1956.
Gogarty, Oliver St. J., *As I was going down Sackville Street.* Rich and Cowan Ltd., London, 1937.
Gray, Tony, *The Irish Answer.* Heinemann, London, 1966.
Harvey, John, *Dublin: A Study in Environment.*

B. T. Batsford Ltd., London, 1949.
Holloway, Joseph, *Abbey Theatre.* Southern Illinois University Press, Illinois, 1967.
Holt, Edgar, *Protest in Arms.* Putnam, London, 1960.
Joyce, James, *Ulysses.* Shakespeare and Company, Paris, 1926.
Kain, Richard M., *Dublin in the Age of W. B. Yeats and James Joyce.* David and Charles, Newton Abbott, 1972.
Kee, Robert, *The Green Flag.* Quartet Books, London, 1976.
Killanin, Lord and Duignan, Michael V., *The Shell Guide to Ireland.* Ebury Press, London, 1967.
Lehane, Brendan, *The Companion Guide to Ireland.* Collins, London, 1973.
Longford, Christine, *A Biography of Dublin.* Methuen & Co. Ltd., London, 1936.
Lyons, F. S. L., *Ireland Since the Famine.* Weidenfeld & Nicolson, London, 1971.
Macardle, Dorothy, *The Irish Republic.* Victor Gollancz Ltd., London, 1938.
MacThomáis, Eamonn and O'Brien, Michael, *Me Jewel and Darlin' Dublin.* The O'Brien Press, Dublin, 1977.
Moody, T. W. and Martin, F. X. (eds), *The Course of Irish History.* The Mercier Press, Cork, 1967.

O'Connor, Frank, *The Backward Look.* Macmillan, London, 1967.
O'Connor, Frank, *Leinster, Munster and Connaught.* Robert Hale Ltd., London, 1950.
O'Connor, Ulick, *Brendan Behan.* Hamish Hamilton, London, 1970.
O'Faolin, Sean, *The Irish.* Penguin Books, London, 1947.
O'Hanlon, Thomas J., *The Irish: Portrait of a People.* Andre Deutsch, London, 1976.
Pakenham, Thomas, *The Year of Liberty.* Hodder and Stoughton, London, 1969.
Pritchett, V. S. and Hofer, Evelyn, *Dublin: A Portrait.* The Bodley Head, London, 1967.
Purcell, Mary, *Matt Talbot and His Times.* Gill & Son, Dublin, 1954.
Ryan, John, *Remembering How We Stood.* Gill and Macmillan, Dublin, 1975.
Somerville & Ross, *Experiences of an Irish R.M.* Everyman's Library, Dent, London, 1969.
Tracy, Honor, *Mind you, I've said nothing!* Methuen & Co. Ltd., London, 1953.
White, Terence de Vere, *Ireland.* Thames and Hudson, London, 1968.
White, Terence de Vere, *Leinster.* Faber & Faber, London, 1968.
Whyte, J. H., *Church & State in Modern Ireland 1926-1970.* Gill and Macmillan Ltd., London and Dublin, 1971.

Credits and Acknowledgements

The editors wish to thank the following for their valuable assistance: Caroline Alcock, London; Joseph Byrne, Irish Tourist Board, Dublin; William Donaldson, London; Osmond Dowling, Dublin Diocesan Press Office, Dublin; Jon Findlater, Arthur Guinness Son & Co., Dublin; Susan Goldblatt, London; Hunting Surveys Ltd., London; Irish Sisters of Charity, Dublin; Irish Statistics Office, Dublin; Arthur Keating, Dublin; A. N. S. Lane, London; Rose Lockwood, London; Eileen McGraw, Dublin Diocesan Press Office, Dublin; Kevin B. Nowlan, University College, Dublin; David Sinclair, London; Edward Taylor, Royal Dublin Society, Dublin; Peter Thursfield, *The Irish Times,* Dublin; John Walker, London; Terence de Vere White, Dublin; Hugo Williams, London; Giles Wordsworth, Dorset.

Sources for pictures in this book are shown below, with the exception of those already credited. Pictures from left to right are separated by commas; from top to bottom by dashes.

Cover—Patrick Ward. *Front end paper*—Laurie Lewis. Pages 4, 6, 7—John McDermott. 10, 11—Map by Hunting Surveys Ltd., London, (Silhouettes by Norman Bancroft-Hunt, Caterham Hill, Surrey). 12, 14, 15—Laurie Lewis. 18 to 20—John McDermott. 24, 25—Laurie Lewis. 26, 27—John McDermott. 28, 29—John McDermott except 29 bottom left—Laurie Lewis. 30—Laurie Lewis. 31 to 45—John McDermott. 46, 47—Courtesy of the Victoria and Albert Museum, London. 48—Steve Herr, London. 50, 51—Laurie Lewis except 50 right—John McDermott. 52, 53—Steve Herr, London. 55, 70—John McDermott. 73—George Morrison Collection, Co. Dublin—The Mansell Collection, London. 77—Steve Herr, London. 80, 81—(top) pics. 1, 2, Laurie Lewis, pics. 3, 4, John McDermott, Laurie Lewis—(middle) pics. 1, 2, Laurie Lewis, Steve Herr, London, Laurie Lewis, John McDermott—(bottom) Laurie Lewis, John McDermott, pics. 3, 4, 5, Laurie Lewis. 82—Laurie Lewis. 84. 85—John McDermott. 87—Radio Times Hulton Picture Library, London. 88—*The Irish Times,* Dublin. 89—Associated Press, London. 91—John McDermott. 94, 95—Syndication International, London. 96—George Morrison Collection, Co. Dublin. 97—Robert Hunt Library, London/National Library of Ireland, Dublin—George Morrison Collection, Co. Dublin. 98 (inset)—George Morrison Collection, Co. Dublin. 98, 99—Popperfoto, London. 100—J. Cashman Collection, Dublin. 101—Old Dublin Society, at Dublin Civic Museum—Popperfoto, London. 102, 103—J. Cashman Collection, Dublin. 104, 107—John McDermott. 108, 110, 111—Steve Herr, London. 112 to 118—John McDermott. 136—Courtesy of the National Gallery of Ireland, Dublin. 139—Courtesy of the Board of Trinity College, Dublin. 140—Laurie Lewis. 142, 143—John McDermott except 143 middle right—Laurie Lewis. 144, 145—Radio Times Hulton Picture Library, London. 146—The Abbey Theatre, Dublin. 148—George Morrison Collection, Co. Dublin. 149—G. A. Duncan, Dublin. 151—Steve Herr, London. 154—Snark International, Paris/courtesy of Mrs. Elizabeth Solterer, Washington, John McDermott. 168, 173—John McDermott. 174—Laurie Lewis. 179—John McDermott. 181, 182, 183—Laurie Lewis. 184, 185—John McDermott. *Last end paper*—Steve Herr, London.

We acknowledge permission to use quotations from the following: "*Gas from a Burner*" by James Joyce by permission of The Society of Authors as the literary representative of the Estate of James Joyce; *The Vanishing Irish* edited by John A. O'Brien by permission of W. H. Allen; *Easter 1916* by W. B. Yeats by permission of A. P. Watt Ltd., *J. M. Synge, Interviews and Recollections* edited by E. H. Mikhail by permission of Macmillan, London and Basingstoke; *As I was going down Sackville Street* by Oliver St. John Gogarty published by Rich and Cowan; *At-Swim-Two-Birds* by Flann O'Brien published by Macgibbon and Kee by permission of the Flann O'Brien Estate; *The Irish* by Donald S. Connery published by Eyre and Spottiswoode by permission of Associated Book Publishers Ltd.

Index

Numerals in italics indicate a photograph or drawing of the subject mentioned.

Colour reproduction by Irwin Photography Ltd., at their Leeds Studio.
Filmsetting by C. E. Dawkins (Typesetters) Ltd., London, SE1 1UN.
Printed and bound in Italy by Arnoldo Mondadori, Verona.